hamlyn cookery club

Chinese
flavours

hamlyn cookery club

Chinese

flavours

First published in 1999 by Hamlyn
an imprint of Octopus Publishing Group Ltd
2–4 Heron Quays
London E14 4JP

British Library Cataloguing-in-Publication Data
A catalogue record for this book is available from the
British Library.

ISBN 0 600 59904 3

Printed in China

Publishing Director: Laura Bamford
Copy Editor: Anne Crane
Creative Director: Keith Martin
Design Manager: Bryan Dunn
Designer: Martin Topping
Jacket Photography: Sean Myers
Picture Researchers: Christine Junemann and Stevie Moe
Senior Production Controller: Katherine Hockley

Notes

1 Both metric and imperial measurements have been given in
all recipes. Use one set of measurements only and not a
mixture of both.
2 Standard level spoon measurements are used in all recipes.
1 tablespoon = one 15 ml spoon
1 teaspoon = one 5 ml spoon
3 Eggs should be medium unless otherwise stated.
4 Milk should be full fat unless otherwise stated.
5 Fresh herbs should be used unless otherwise stated.
If unavailable use dried herbs as an alternative but halve the
quantities stated.
6 Pepper should be freshly ground black pepper unless
otherwise stated.
7 Ovens should be preheated to the specified temperature
– if using a fan-assisted oven, follow the manufacturer's
instructions for adjusting the time and temperature.
8 Measurements for canned food have been given as a
standard metric equivalent.

Contents

Introduction

It is said that if you ate a different Chinese dish every day for twenty years, there would still be more to come – a happy thought for lovers of Chinese food. The over 100 recipes selected for this book have all been chosen for their tastiness and ease of preparation, and in some cases adapted to the western kitchen. The more exotic ingredients, described in the list opposite, can all be found in Chinese and Asian shops and with increasing ease in large supermarkets.

Planning and Serving a Chinese Meal

At a Chinese meal all the dishes are put on the table at the same time. Each person has a dinner plate, a bowl for rice and soup, a porcelain spoon and a pair of chopsticks. A meal for two or three people will include a meat dish, a vegetable dish, a soup and a rice dish. For an informal meal for four or six people, serve four dishes, plus soup and rice. For a formal meal, serve six or eight dishes. When cooking for more people, increase the number of dishes rather than the quantities.

When deciding what to cook, choose two, or at most three, stir-fried dishes, which must be served immediately, together with steamed, braised or roasted dishes.

Most Chinese recipes can also be served in western style, either on their own or with western dishes. Many of the dishes in this book are shown with traditional garnishes; these are not essential but look very effective, if you have enough time.

Cooking Methods and Equipment

Stir-frying, which involves cooking foods in a small quantity of very hot oil over a very high heat, is the best-known Chinese cooking method. Since it is so speedy, it is essential that all the ingredients are sliced or shredded to an even size in advance, and that all the necessary sauces and spices are to hand. Slicing on the diagonal, which exposes a larger area to the heat than straight slices, is a favourite Chinese technique. A wok is essential for effective stir-frying and is also used in China for deep-frying, braising and for steaming in conjunction with a traditional bamboo steamer. However, a western metal steamer will do equally well.

Special Ingredients

Bamboo shoots
Cream coloured and crunchy, these are available in cans.

Bean curd
Also known as tofu, this is made from ground yellow soya beans and high in protein. It is almost tasteless so takes on the flavour of the ingredients cooked with it. There is a soft variety, also known as silken tofu, which is good for soups and a firm version which is used for stir-frying and braising.

Bean sprouts
The crunchy sprouts of the mung bean, these can be kept in the refrigerator for 2–3 days.
The canned variety is a poor substitute for the fresh version.

Black beans
Salted, fermented soya beans with a very strong salty flavour. Sold in cans and plastic packs.

Cooking oil
Groundnut (peanut) oil is the Chinese choice.

Dried Chinese mushrooms (including wood ears and cloud ears)
Widely used for their flavour and aroma, these mushrooms must be soaked in warm water for 20–30 minutes before use.

Five-spice powder
A highly piquant mixture of star anise, fennel seeds, cloves, cinnamon and Sichuan pepper.

Ginger
Fresh root ginger is sold by weight in the vegetable section of supermarkets. Peel and slice or chop it finely before use. Store in the refrigerator. Ground ginger is not a suitable substitute.

Hoisin sauce
This pungent condiment, also known as barbecue sauce, is widely available from supermarkets, or you can make your own (see page 58).

Noodles
Cellophane or transparent noodles are made from ground mung beans. Soak in warm water for 5 minutes before use.
Egg noodles are made from wheat flour and egg and are sold both fresh and dried. Cook according to packet instructions.
Rice noodles are also available fresh and dried. Dried noodles need to be soaked before use; fresh noodles can be used straightaway. Rice vermicelli are very fine rice noodles.

Oyster sauce
A thick brown sauce made from oysters and soy sauce.

Sichuan pickled or preserved vegetables
The root of a variety of mustard green pickled in salt and hot chillies. Sold in cans, it must be rinsed and sliced before use, and gives a hot, crunchy texture and spicy flavour to dishes.

Sesame seed oil
Sold in bottles and used in China as a garnish rather than as a cooking oil. Buy the Chinese version and not the refined yellow sesame oil sold in Middle Eastern stores.

Soy sauce
Made from fermented and salted soya beans, this comes in various strengths and degrees of saltiness. Light soy sauces tend to be thinner and saltier than dark ones.

Water chestnuts
Crisp, white and crunchy, these are usually sold canned but can occasionally be found fresh in supermarkets and Chinese grocers.

Soups

Hot Peppery Soup

2 bean curd (tofu) cakes
2 tablespoons oil
2 red or green chillies, deseeded and chopped
125 g (4 oz) chicken breast, minced
1 tablespoon cornflour
8 crisp lettuce leaves
900 ml (1½ pints) chicken stock
2 tablespoons soy sauce
2 spring onions, chopped
125 g (4 oz) cooked peeled prawns
1 tablespoon cider vinegar
pepper

Cut each bean curd cake into 10 pieces. Heat the oil in a wok or frying pan, add the chillies and fry for about 30 seconds to extract the flavour; then discard them. Add the bean curd to the wok and fry for 3–4 minutes until golden brown. Drain and set aside.

Mix the chicken and cornflour. Tear each lettuce leaf into pieces.

Heat the stock, add the chicken and cornflour mixture and stir. Add the lettuce, soy sauce, spring onions, prawns and cider vinegar. Bring to the boil, then add pepper to taste. Cook for 2 minutes. Then add the bean curd and serve hot.

Serves 4–6

Sweetcorn and Prawn Soup

2 teaspoons finely chopped fresh root ginger
1 tablespoon dry sherry
250 g (8 oz) cooked peeled prawns
900 ml (1½ pints) chicken stock
375 g (12 oz) can sweetcorn, drained
50 g (2 oz) lean ham, diced
1 tablespoon chopped chives
salt

Mix together the ginger, sherry and prawns. Bring the stock to the boil, then stir in the prawn mixture. Add the sweetcorn to the pan with salt to taste. Cook for 2 minutes, stirring occasionally.

Sprinkle with the ham and chives and serve immediately.

Serves 4–6

Pork Spare Rib Soup

500 g (1 lb) pork spare ribs
1 tablespoon oil
2 teaspoons shredded fresh root ginger
1 garlic clove, sliced
2 spring onions, chopped
900 ml (1½ pints) beef stock
1 teaspoon salt
2 tomatoes, diced
250 g (8 oz) bean sprouts

Cut the spare ribs into 2.5 cm (1 inch) pieces.

Heat the oil in a saucepan, add the spare ribs and fry for 5 minutes until golden brown. Add the ginger, garlic and spring onions and cook for 2 minutes. Add the stock, season and bring to the boil. Cover and simmer for 1 hour or until the spare ribs are tender.

Add the tomatoes and the bean sprouts and cook for 1 minute. Serve hot.

Serves 4–6

top right: hot peppery soup;
middle: sweetcorn and prawn soup;
bottom right: pork spare rib soup

Shredded Pork and Noodles in Soup

3–4 dried Chinese mushrooms
  (optional)
250 g (8 oz) lean pork, shredded
1 tablespoon soy sauce
1 tablespoon dry sherry
375 g (12 oz) egg noodles
900 ml (1½ pints) chicken stock
4 spring onions, chopped
125 g (4 oz) canned bamboo shoots,
  drained and shredded
a few Chinese cabbage leaves,
  shredded

Soak the mushrooms, if using, in warm water for 15 minutes. Squeeze dry, discard the hard stalks, then slice the mushroom caps.

Put the pork into a bowl, add the soy sauce and sherry and leave to marinate for 10–15 minutes.

Cook the noodles in lightly salted boiling water for about 5 minutes, or until cooked; drain thoroughly.

Bring the stock to the boil in a large saucepan, add the mushrooms, if using, the pork with the marinade, spring onions and bamboo shoots. Simmer for 2–3 minutes, then add the noodles and shredded cabbage. Cook for 2 minutes. Serve hot.

Serves 4–6

Velvet Chicken and Mushroom Soup

175 g (6 oz) chicken breast
1 egg white
2 teaspoons cornflour
900 ml (1½ pints) chicken stock
50 g (2 oz) button mushrooms, sliced
75 g (3 oz) canned bamboo shoots,
  drained and shredded
1 teaspoon finely chopped fresh root
  ginger
2 spring onions, chopped
½ teaspoon salt
1 tablespoon soy sauce

Cut the chicken into matchstick pieces. Put the egg white and cornflour into a bowl and mix well. Add the chicken and toss until evenly coated.

Bring the stock to the boil, add the chicken, mushrooms, bamboo shoots, ginger, spring onions, salt and soy sauce and simmer gently for 3 minutes. Serve hot.

Serves 4–6

Pure Vegetable Soup

4 dried Chinese mushrooms
25 g (1 oz) transparent noodles
½ bunch of watercress
900 ml (1½ pints) chicken stock
2 courgettes, diced
1 small turnip, diced
50 g (2 oz) spinach, chopped
2 carrots, diced
1 teaspoon salt
1 tablespoon soy sauce
2 spring onions, chopped

Soak the mushrooms in warm water for 15 minutes. Squeeze dry and discard the hard stalks, then slice the mushroom caps.

Soak the noodles in hot water for 10 minutes; drain. Remove the stalks from the watercress and separate the leaves.

Bring the stock to the boil in a large saucepan. Add the courgettes, turnip, watercress, spinach and carrots and simmer for 20 minutes.

Add the salt, soy sauce and spring onions and cook for 5 minutes. Serve hot.

Serves 4–6

*top left: shredded pork and noodles in soup; **middle**: velvet chicken and mushroom soup; **bottom left**: pure vegetable soup*

Hot and Sour Soup

4 dried Chinese mushrooms
2 celery sticks
900 ml (1½ pints) chicken stock
175 g (6 oz) cooked peeled prawns
50 g (2 oz) Sichuan pickled vegetable, sliced
50 g (2 oz) canned bamboo shoots, drained and shredded
½ cucumber
2 tablespoons sherry
2 tablespoons soy sauce
1 tablespoon red wine vinegar
25 g (1 oz) ham, diced
1 spring onion, chopped

Soak the mushrooms in warm water for 15 minutes. Squeeze dry, discard the hard stalks, then slice the mushroom caps. Slice the celery sticks diagonally.

Bring the stock to the boil in a large saucepan, add the prawns, pickled vegetables, bamboo shoots, mushrooms and celery and simmer for 5 minutes.

Cut the cucumber into 5 cm (2 inch) matchsticks. Add to the pan with the sherry, soy sauce, vinegar and ham and cook for 1 minute. Sprinkle with the spring onion and serve immediately.

Serves 4–6

Spinach and Bean Curd Soup

Serve crisp fried noodles or prawn crackers to add variety of texture when you make this soup.

900 ml (1½ pints) chicken stock
2 green chillies, deseeded and sliced
1 red pepper, cored, deseeded and cut into strips
500 g (1 lb) fresh spinach leaves, shredded
1 bunch of spring onions, chopped
1 tablespoon cornflour
2 tablespoons water
125 g (4 oz) chicken (reserved from the stock if making), diced
250 g (8 oz) bean curd (tofu), sliced
salt and pepper

left: hot and sour soup

Pour the chicken stock into a wok and bring it slowly to the boil. Add the sliced chillies and red pepper strips, and salt and pepper to taste, then simmer for 5 minutes. Stir in the spinach and spring onions and cook for a further 2–3 minutes.

Meanwhile, blend the cornflour with the water until smooth, then stir this into the soup. Bring the soup to the boil, simmer gently for 2 minutes, then stir in the chopped chicken and the bean curd. Heat through without boiling, then serve the soup from the wok or ladle into individual bowls.

Serves 4

Clam and Abalone Soup with Chinese Mushrooms

8–10 dried Chinese mushrooms

1.2 litres (2 pints) chicken or
   vegetable stock

50 g (2 oz) canned abalone, thinly
   sliced

125 g (4 oz) chicken breast, thinly
   sliced

2.5 cm (1 inch) piece fresh root
   ginger, peeled and diced

1–2 tablespoons dry sherry

1 tablespoon soy sauce

250 g (8 oz) can clams, drained

chopped spring onion, to garnish

Soak the mushrooms in warm water for 15 minutes. Squeeze dry and discard the hard stalks, then cut the mushroom caps into quarters.

Bring the stock to the boil and add the abalone, chicken and ginger. Simmer for 2 minutes, then add the sherry, soy sauce and clams and cook for 2 minutes.

Sprinkle the soup with the spring onion and serve immediately.

Serves 4–6

above: clam and abalone soup with chinese mushrooms

Egg Flower Soup

4–5 dried Chinese mushrooms

2 tablespoons soy sauce

2 teaspoons cornflour

175 g (6 oz) pork fillet, shredded

900 ml (1½ pints) chicken stock

1 teaspoon salt

2 eggs

2 spring onions, chopped

1 tablespoon chopped coriander

Soak the dried mushrooms in warm water for 10 minutes. Rinse and drain well, then chop roughly.

Blend together the soy sauce and cornflour. Add the pork and toss until evenly coated. Bring the stock to the boil, add the salt, pork and mushrooms and cook for 5 minutes.

Beat the eggs until frothy and pour them into the boiling stock, stirring constantly. Remove the pan from the heat, add the spring onions and coriander and serve.

Serves 4–6

Soup with Beef Balls

4–5 dried Chinese mushrooms

375 g (12 oz) lean beef, minced

1 onion, finely chopped

1 tablespoon cornflour

1 small egg

900 ml (1½ pints) beef or chicken stock

1 bunch of watercress, stalks removed

3 spring onions, finely chopped

1 tablespoon soy sauce

salt

Soak the mushrooms in a bowl of warm water for 15 minutes. Squeeze dry and discard the hard stalks, then slice the mushroom caps.

Mix the beef, onion, salt to taste, cornflour and egg together and shape the mixture into small balls. Drop the meat balls into iced water for 15 minutes; drain thoroughly.

Meanwhile, heat the stock in a large pan. Add the meat balls and cook for 10 minutes. Add the mushrooms, watercress, spring onions and soy sauce and cook the soup for 2 minutes. Serve hot.

Serves 4–6

above: egg flower soup; soup with beef balls

Wonton Soup

Serve this substantial soup as a main dish. Ready-made wonton skins can be bought from Asian shops.

175 g (6 oz) minced pork
125 g (4 oz) fresh spinach leaves, chopped
½ teaspoon salt
1 teaspoon sugar
1 tablespoon sherry
24 ready-made wonton skins
600 ml (1 pint) chicken stock
1 spring onion, finely chopped, to garnish

Mix the minced pork and chopped spinach leaves with the salt, sugar and sherry.

Place 1 teaspoon of the meat and spinach mixture in the centre of each wonton skin. Bring the opposite corners of the wonton together in a fold. Seal by pinching the top edges together firmly with your fingers. Fold the other two corners towards each other and seal in the same way.

Bring the stock to the boil, drop in the wontons and boil the soup rapidly for 2–3 minutes. Serve hot in individual bowls, garnished with chopped spring onions.

Serves 4

right: wonton soup

Chicken and Sweetcorn Soup

Serve crisp prawn crackers to complement this soup if you like.

900 ml (1½ pints) chicken stock
375 g (12 oz) sweetcorn
2 teaspoons cornflour (optional)
1 tablespoon water (optional)
2 cooked chicken joints, shredded
salt and pepper
chopped spring onions, to garnish (optional)

Pour the stock into a wok and add 250 g (8 oz) of the sweetcorn. Bring to the boil, season to taste with salt and pepper and simmer, covered, for 15 minutes. Blend the soup in a liquidizer until smooth, then return it to the wok.

Reheat the soup and decide whether it is thick enough for your liking. If not, blend the cornflour with the water and stir it into the soup, then bring to the boil. Add the remaining sweetcorn and the chicken. Simmer for 5 minutes, then taste and adjust the seasoning if necessary. Serve garnished with spring onions.

Serves 4

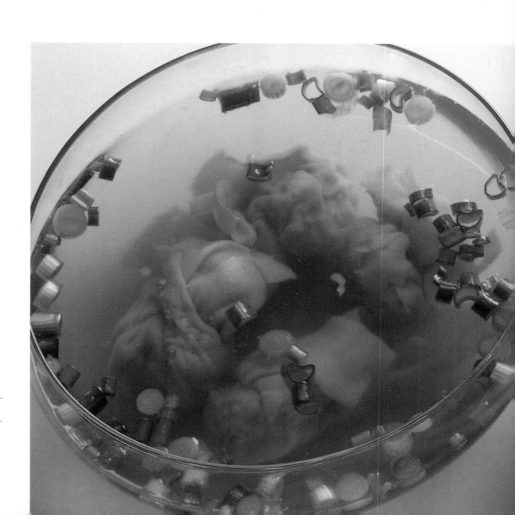

Fish and Shellfish

Deep-fried Scallops

12 scallops

½ teaspoon very finely chopped fresh
   root ginger

2 spring onions, finely chopped

3 tablespoons self-raising flour

a pinch of salt

2 teaspoons dry sherry

1 egg, beaten

oil, for deep-frying

To garnish:

tomato flower (optional)

coriander leaves

Cut the scallops in half and cook in boiling water for 1 minute; drain thoroughly. Mix the scallops with the ginger and spring onions.

Put the flour and salt in a bowl, add the sherry and egg and beat to a smooth batter. Fold in the scallops and toss until evenly coated.

Heat the oil in a wok or deep-fryer to 160°C (325°F) and deep-fry the scallops for 2–3 minutes until golden brown. Drain thoroughly on kitchen paper.

Arrange the scallops on a warmed serving dish and garnish with a tomato flower, if using, and coriander leaves. Serve immediately.

Serves 4

Quick-fried Prawns

125 g (4 oz) fresh asparagus, cut into
   2.5 cm (1 inch) pieces (optional)

4 tablespoons dry sherry

1 egg white

500 g (1 lb) peeled raw prawns

1 tablespoon oil

1 teaspoon finely chopped fresh root
   ginger

2 spring onions, chopped

salt

Cook the asparagus, if using, in boiling salted water for 5 minutes; drain thoroughly.

Mix 2 tablespoons of the sherry with the egg white and a pinch of salt. Add the prawns and toss until evenly coated; drain.

Heat the oil in a wok or frying pan, add the ginger and half of the spring onions and fry for 2 minutes. Add the prawns and cook for about 5 minutes, or until they become pink. Add the asparagus, if using, and the remaining sherry and cook for 1 minute.

Transfer to a warmed serving dish and sprinkle with the remaining spring onion. Serve immediately.

Serves 4–6

Paper-wrapped Fish

4 plaice or sole fillets, each weighing
   125 g (4 oz)
a pinch of salt
2 tablespoons dry sherry
1 tablespoon oil
2 tablespoons shredded spring onion
2 tablespoons shredded root ginger
oil, for deep-frying
spring onion flowers, to garnish
   (optional)

Cut the fish fillets into 2.5 cm (1 inch) squares. Sprinkle with salt and toss in the sherry.

Cut out 15 cm (6 inch) squares of greaseproof paper and brush with the oil. Place a piece of fish on each square of paper and arrange some shredded spring onion and ginger on top. Fold into envelopes tucking in the flaps to secure.

Heat the oil in a wok or deep-fryer to 180°C (350°F). Deep-fry the wrapped fish for 3 minutes. Drain the parcels on kitchen paper and arrange on a warmed serving dish. Garnish with spring onion flowers, if using, and serve immediately. Each person unwraps his own parcels at the table with chopsticks.

Serves 4

above: paper-wrapped fish

Quick-fried Squid with Crab and Tomato Sauce

500 g (1 lb) cleaned squid, cut into
  2.5 cm (1 inch) pieces
1 tablespoon oil
2 x 2.5 cm (1 inch) pieces fresh root
  ginger, peeled and finely chopped
3 spring onions, finely chopped
175 g (6 oz) can crab meat
65 g (2 ½ oz) can tomato purée
1 teaspoon sugar
1 tablespoon light soy sauce
4 tablespoons chicken stock
1 tablespoon dry sherry
2 teaspoons cornflour
1 tablespoon water
chopped spring onion, to garnish

Heat the oil in a wok or deep frying pan, add the ginger and spring onions and stir-fry for 1 minute. Add the squid, stir-fry for 2 more minutes, then add the remaining ingredients, except the cornflour and water, and mix well. Cook for 2 further minutes, stirring.

Blend the cornflour and water to a smooth paste and stir into the pan and cook, stirring, to thicken.

Spoon the mixture into a warmed serving dish, garnish with spring onion and serve immediately.

Serves 4–6

Quick-fried Crab in Aromatic Oil

1 large freshly cooked crab or
  2 x 175 g (6 oz) canned crab meat
2 tablespoons oil
1 garlic clove, crushed
2 x 2.5 cm (1 inch) pieces fresh root
  ginger, peeled and finely chopped
4 spring onions, chopped
1 leek, thinly sliced
1 egg, beaten
150 ml (¼ pint) fish or chicken stock
2 tablespoons dry sherry
2 teaspoons cornflour, blended with
  1 tablespoon water
2 teaspoons sesame seed oil
salt
lemon wedges, to garnish

If using a fresh crab, break off the legs and crack the claws. Using a chopper, crack the shell into about 4–5 pieces. Remove all the meat and cut it into pieces, discarding the black sac and intestinal thread.

Heat the oil in a wok, add the garlic, ginger and spring onions and stir-fry for 1 minute. Add the crab and stir-fry for 5 minutes over a high heat. Add the leek and season.

Lower the heat and pour in the egg in a thin stream. Add the stock and sherry and cook for 1 minute. Add the cornflour and the sesame oil and cook, stirring, until thickened.

Serve immediately, garnished with lemon wedges.

Serves 4–6

Sautéed Prawns in Sauce

500 g (1 lb) Pacific prawns, shelled
  and deveined
½ teaspoon salt
2 teaspoons dry sherry
1 egg white
1 tablespoon cornflour
5 tablespoons vegetable oil
½ teaspoon crushed garlic
3 spring onions, cut into 2.5 cm
  (1 inch) pieces
1 tablespoon soy sauce
1 teaspoon sugar
1 tablespoon red wine vinegar
a dash of Tabasco sauce

Cut the prawns into 2.5 cm (1 inch) pieces. Mix together the salt, sherry, egg white and cornflour in a large bowl. Add the prawns and toss to coat with the batter.

Heat the oil in a wok or frying pan. Add the garlic, prawns and spring onions and stir-fry for 2 minutes. Add the soy sauce, sugar, vinegar and Tabasco sauce and stir well. Serve hot.

Serves 4

right: quick-fried squid with crab and tomato sauce; far right: quick-fried crab in aromatic oil

Deep-fried Spiced Fish

750 g (1½ lb) whole fish (sole, cod, snapper), cleaned and scaled
1 teaspoon grated fresh root ginger
3 spring onions, chopped
2 teaspoons salt
2 tablespoons dry sherry
oil, for deep-frying
1 teaspoon ground Sichuan or black peppercorns
2 tablespoons sesame seed oil

To garnish:
lemon slices
parsley sprigs
chopped spring onion
glacé cherry quarters (optional)

Make diagonal slashes on each side of the fish. Place the ginger, spring onions, 1 teaspoon of the salt and the sherry in a shallow dish and add the fish. Cover and leave to marinate for 30 minutes.

Heat the oil in a wok or deep-fryer to 180°C (350°F). Deep-fry the fish until golden brown. Drain the fish on kitchen paper and place on a warmed serving dish. Sprinkle with the ground peppercorns and remaining salt. Heat the sesame seed oil and pour it over the fish. Serve immediately, garnished with the lemon slices, parsley, chopped spring onion and glacé cherry quarters, if using.

Serves 6

Steamed Whole Fish

The Chinese like to cook their fish whole with the head and tail intact. You will need a bamboo steamer not less than 33 cm (13 inches) in diameter in order to take a plate 30 cm (12 inches) long. Otherwise, halve the fish and use a round dish which will fit into a Western metal steamer.

2 Chinese dried mushrooms
500 g (1 lb) whole fish (sea bass or perch), scaled and cleaned
2 x 2.5 cm (1 inch) slices fresh root ginger, peeled
2 spring onions

50 g (2 oz) cooked ham
50 g (2 oz) bamboo shoots
3 tablespoons dry sherry
2 tablespoons soy sauce
1 teaspoon sugar
1 teaspoon salt

Soak the mushrooms in warm water for 20 minutes, squeeze them dry and discard the stalks.

Slash both sides of the fish diagonally as deep as the bone at intervals of about 1 cm (½ inch). This prevents the skin from bursting in cooking, allows the heat to penetrate more quickly and helps to diffuse the flavour of the seasonings and sauce. Dry the fish well, then put it on a plate.

Thinly shred the root ginger, spring onions, ham, mushrooms and bamboo shoots, then arrange them evenly on top of the fish. Mix the sherry, soy sauce, sugar and salt in a jug and pour this sauce over the fish. Steam vigorously for 15 minutes. Serve accompanied with steamed vegetables, if liked.

Serves 4

Braised Fish

1 x 625 g (1¼ lb) fish (sea bass, grey mullet, carp, perch), scaled and cleaned
3 tablespoons oil
2 x 2.5 cm (1 inch) slices root ginger, peeled and thinly shredded
1 spring onion, cut into 2.5 cm (1 inch) pieces
Sauce:
3 tablespoons dry sherry
3 tablespoons soy sauce
1 teaspoon sugar
½ teaspoon salt
2 tablespoons fish stock or water
½ teaspoon five-spice powder (optional)

Divide the fish by cutting it into about 4 pieces.

Heat the oil until hot in a large heavy frying pan or wok, then fry the fish for 5 minutes, turning the pieces once. Move the fish to one side and fry the shredded ginger and spring onion. Mix together all the sauce ingredients and add them to the pan.

Return the fish to the middle of the pan. Simmer for 10 minutes, turning the fish pieces over once, very carefully, halfway through cooking. This dish can be served either hot or cold.

Serves 4

far left: steamed whole fish;
left: braised fish

Cantonese Whole Fish

4 dried Chinese mushrooms
1–1.25 kg (2–2½ lb) whole fish (trout, mullet, bass) cleaned
2 x 2.5 cm (1 inch) pieces fresh root ginger, peeled
2 spring onions

50 g (2 oz) cooked ham
50 g (2 oz) canned bamboo shoots, drained
sliced cucumber, to garnish

Marinade:
1 garlic clove, sliced
3 tablespoons soy sauce
2 tablespoons dry sherry
2 tablespoons chicken stock
2 teaspoons cornflour

Soak the mushrooms in warm water for 15 minutes. Squeeze dry, discard the hard stalks, then slice the mushroom caps.

Score the flesh of the fish by making 3 diagonal cuts on each side. Place in a shallow dish.

Mix together all the marinade ingredients and spoon over the fish. Cover and leave to marinate for at least 30 minutes.

Finely shred the ginger, spring onions, ham and bamboo shoots, then mix with the mushrooms.

Place the fish on a heatproof plate. Pour over the marinade and place in a steamer. Sprinkle with the mushroom mixture and steam vigorously for 15–20 minutes, until tender. Transfer to a warmed serving platter and serve garnished with the cucumber slices.

Serves 4–6

Five-spice Battered Prawns

This is also a tasty way of preparing frozen prawns. Defrost and dry the prawns thoroughly before coating them with the batter.

4 tablespoons self-raising flour
a pinch of salt
½ teaspoon five-spice powder
2.5 cm (1 inch) piece fresh root
   ginger, peeled and finely chopped
1 egg
4–5 tablespoons water
500 g (1 lb) giant Pacific prawns,
   shelled
oil, for deep-frying
To garnish:
shredded spring onions
lemon twists

Sift the flour, salt and five-spice powder into a mixing bowl, then add the ginger. Make a hollow in the centre and add the egg. Beat thoroughly, adding sufficient water to make a smooth light batter.

Heat the oil in a deep-fryer. Dip each prawn into the batter, then deep-fry 2 or 3 prawns at a time for 2–3 minutes, until golden brown. Drain the prawns on kitchen paper and keep warm.

Arrange on a warmed serving dish and garnish with spring onions and lemon. Serve immediately.

Serves 4–6

Soy Fish Steak

500 g (1 lb) fish steak (cod or
   halibut)
½ teaspoon salt
2 tablespoons sherry
4 tablespoons cornflour
1 egg white, beaten
3 tablespoons oil
1 slice fresh root ginger, peeled and
   finely chopped
2 tablespoons soy sauce
2 teaspoons sugar
120 ml (4 fl oz) fish stock or water
spring onion, to garnish

Cut the fish steak into bite-sized pieces. Mix together the salt, sherry and 1 tablespoon of the cornflour in a shallow dish, then marinate the fish, covered, for about 30 minutes. Dip the marinated fish pieces in egg white, then coat them with the remaining cornflour.

Heat the oil in a wok or frying pan until hot, then fry the fish pieces until golden, stirring very gently to separate each piece. Add the ginger, soy sauce, sugar and fish stock or water, then cook for about 3–4 minutes or until the liquid is entirely evaporated. Serve hot garnished with the spring onion.

Serves 4

top left: cantonese whole fish;
bottom left: *five-spice battered prawns;* ***above:*** *soy fish steak*

Steamed Sweet and Sour Fish

1 large whole plaice, cleaned

2 pieces fresh root ginger, shredded

3 spring onions, sliced

salt

Sauce:

150 ml (¼ pint) fish or chicken stock

1 tablespoon soy sauce

1 tablespoon sugar

1 tablespoon wine vinegar

1 tablespoon dry sherry

1 tablespoon tomato purée

1 teaspoon chilli sauce

a pinch of salt

1 tablespoon cornflour

2 tablespoons water

lemon slices or tomato flowers,
  to garnish (optional)

Make 3 diagonal cuts on each side of the fish. Rub the fish with salt and sprinkle with the ginger and spring onions. Put the fish on an ovenproof plate and place in a steamer. Steam for 12–15 minutes or until tender.

Meanwhile, make the sauce. Mix all the sauce ingredients, except the cornflour and water in a saucepan, bring to the boil and cook for 1 minute. Blend the cornflour with the water and stir it into the sauce. Cook, stirring, until thickened.

Carefully transfer the steamed fish on to a warmed serving dish. Spoon over the sauce and serve hot. Garnish each individual plate with lemon slices and tomato flowers, if liked.

Serves 4

Braised Fish with Black Beans

3 tablespoons black beans
2 tablespoons oil
2 spring onions, chopped
1 piece fresh root ginger, peeled and
  finely chopped
1 small red pepper, cored, deseeded
  and diced
2 celery sticks, chopped

2 tablespoons soy sauce
2 tablespoons dry sherry
4 cod or haddock cutlets, each
  weighing 150 g (5 oz)
shredded spring onion, to garnish

Soak the black beans in warm water for about 10 minutes. Drain well.

Heat the oil in a wok or deep frying pan, add the spring onions, ginger, red pepper and celery and stir-fry for 1 minute. Stir in the soy sauce and sherry. Place the fish on top of the vegetables and simmer for about 5–10 minutes until almost tender, depending on the thickness of the fish. Spoon over the black beans and cook for 2 minutes.

Arrange the fish on a warmed serving dish and spoon over the sauce. Serve hot, garnished with spring onion.

Serves 4

Trout with Salted Cabbage

2 tablespoons oil

1 onion, chopped

2 x 2.5 cm (1 inch) pieces fresh root ginger, peeled and finely shredded

4 trout, cleaned

150 ml (¼ pint) chicken stock

25 g (1 oz) pickled cabbage, chopped

25 g (1 oz) canned bamboo shoots, drained and sliced

1 tablespoon soy sauce

2 teaspoons dry sherry

To garnish:

lemon twists

coriander leaves

Heat the oil in a wok or deep frying pan, add the onion and ginger and cook for 1 minute. Add the trout and fry for 1 minute on each side, until browned.

Stir in the stock, then add the cabbage, bamboo shoots, soy sauce and sherry. Cook for 10 minutes, basting the fish occasionally.

Transfer to a warmed serving dish and garnish with lemon twists topped with coriander leaves. Serve immediately.

Serves 4

top left: trout with salted cabbage;
bottom left: five-willow fish;
right: soft noodles with crab meat sauce

Five-willows Fish

1 grey mullet, carp or bass, cleaned
4 tablespoons oil
1 tablespoon hoisin sauce
2 tablespoons sugar
1 tablespoon sesame seed oil
Marinade:
1 small cucumber, halved lengthways
2 carrots
2.5 cm (1 inch) piece fresh root
   ginger, sliced
3 spring onions, chopped
2 garlic cloves, 1 crushed and 1 sliced
120 ml (4 fl oz) vinegar
To garnish:
cucumber fan
carrot flower

Discard the soft centre of the
cucumber and slice the cucumber
and the carrots into matchsticks.

Put the cucumber, carrots, ginger,
spring onions, crushed garlic and
vinegar into a bowl and mix well.
Cover and marinate for 30 minutes.

Make 3 diagonal cuts on both
sides of the fish. Heat the oil in a
wok or frying pan, add the garlic
and fry for 1 minute. Add the fish
and fry for 5 minutes on each side
until golden brown and cooked.

Add the vegetables and marinade,
stir in the hoisin sauce and sugar
and cook for 2 minutes; sprinkle
with the sesame seed oil.

Transfer the fish to a warmed dish
and spoon over the sauce. Garnish
with cucumber and carrot.

Serves 4–6

Soft Noodles with Crab Meat Sauce

150 g (5 oz) egg noodles
2 tablespoons oil
1 small can crab meat (about 125 g
   (4 oz) drained weight)
125 g (4 oz) Chinese greens, spinach
   or cabbage, roughly chopped
1 teaspoon soy sauce
250 ml (8 fl oz) fish stock
salt
1 spring onion, finely chopped,
   to garnish

Add the noodles to a saucepan of
lightly salted boiling water and boil
for about 5 minutes or according to
packet instructions. Drain them
through a colander, then transfer to
a serving dish and keep warm.

Heat the oil in a wok or large
frying pan, add the crab meat and
greens and stir-fry for 2 minutes.
Add the soy sauce and stock. Cook
for a further 2–3 minutes, then pour
the crab mixture over the noodles.
Transfer to a warmed serving dish
and garnish with the spring onion.
Serve at once.

Serves 2–3

Braised Carp

If the carp is under 1 kg (2 lb) in weight, it is best cooked whole, otherwise it should be cut into 2–3 pieces.

1 kg (2 lb) carp, scaled and cleaned
1 teaspoon salt
2 garlic cloves, crushed
2 slices fresh root ginger, peeled and thinly sliced
4 spring onions, cut into 2.5cm (1 inch) lengths
250 ml (8 fl oz) oil
2 tablespoons soy sauce
1 tablespoon dry sherry
1½ teaspoons sugar
300 ml (½ pint) fish stock or water
1 teaspoon cornflour

To garnish:
shredded spring onion
lemon quarters
glacé cherry

Slash both sides of the fish diagonally, down to the bone, at intervals of about 1 cm (½ inch). Dry the fish and rub the salt on the inside and outside of the fish.

Heat the oil in a wok or deep frying pan until hot, then fry the carp for 2 minutes on each side. Remove the fish from the wok and pour off the excess oil, but leave about 1 tablespoon of oil in the pan. Add the garlic, ginger and spring onions and fry quickly, stirring, for just a few seconds.

Return the fish to the pan, add the soy sauce, sherry, sugar and stock or water and simmer for 10–15 minutes. Mix the cornflour with a little cold water, and add to the pan, stirring constantly. Serve garnished with the spring onion, lemon and cherry.

Serves 4

Braised Prawns in Shells

To make spring onion curls, cut the spring onions very finely and soak in ice cold water until the spring onions curl.

250 g (8 oz) Pacific or tiger prawns
3 tablespoons oil
1 spring onion, cut into short
   lengths

3 slices fresh root ginger, peeled and
   thinly sliced
spring onion curls, to garnish
Sauce:
2 tablespoons soy sauce
2 tablespoons sherry
½ teaspoon salt
1 teaspoon sugar
1 teaspoon cornflour
1 teaspoon cold water

Pull the antennae and legs off of the prawns but leave on the shells.

Combine all the sauce ingredients in a jug and mix well.

Heat the oil in a frying pan or wok until hot, then add the spring onion, ginger and prawns and stir well. Pour the sauce into the pan. Blend well, and cook for 5 minutes or just until the sauce is almost completely evaporated. Garnish with the spring onion curls and serve hot.

Serves 4

Chicken and Duck

Pleasure-boat Duck

2 kg (4 lb) oven-ready duck
4 dried Chinese mushrooms
2 tablespoons oil
4 spring onions, chopped
2.5 cm (1 inch) piece fresh root
   ginger, peeled and finely chopped
125 g (4 oz) lean pork, shredded
50 g (2 oz) broad beans, cooked
Glaze:
3 tablespoons soy sauce
1 tablespoon dry sherry
1 tablespoon sesame seed oil
To garnish:
turnip flowers
radishes
mint leaves

Immerse the duck in a pan of
boiling water for 2 minutes, then
drain well.

Soak the dried mushrooms in
warm water for 15 minutes. Squeeze
dry, discard the hard stalks, then
slice the mushroom caps.

Heat the oil in a wok or frying
pan, add the spring onions, ginger
and pork and fry for 2 minutes. Add
the beans and cook for 1 further
minute. Add the mushrooms.

Leave to cool, then stuff the duck
with the mixture. Sew up securely.

Mix the glaze ingredients together
and brush over the duck. Place in a
roasting tin and cook in a preheated
hot oven, 220°C (425°F), Gas Mark
7, for 1¼–1½ hours, basting
occasionally with the glaze.

Transfer the duck to a warmed
serving dish and garnish with
turnip flowers with radish centres,
and mint leaves. Serve immediately.

Serves 4–6

Soy-braised Duck

1.5–2 kg (3–4 lb) oven-ready duck
4 pieces fresh root ginger, peeled and
   finely chopped
1 large onion, finely chopped
1 teaspoon salt
6 tablespoons soy sauce
3 tablespoons malt vinegar
1 tablespoon oil
4 spring onions, each cut into
   3 pieces
150 ml (¼ pint) chicken stock
250 g (8 oz) can pineapple slices,
   halved
3 tablespoons dry sherry
1 tablespoon cornflour, blended with
   2 tablespoons water
To garnish:
pineapple slices
shredded spring onions

Prick the skin of the duck all over.
Mix the ginger and onion with the
salt and rub it on the inside and
outside of the duck. Place the duck
into a large bowl and add the soy
sauce and vinegar. Cover and leave
for 1 hour, basting occasionally.

Transfer the duck to a roasting pan and cook in a preheated hot oven, 220°C (425°F), Gas Mark 7, for 30 minutes.

Heat the oil in a pan, add the spring onions and fry until lightly browned. Remove and set aside.

Remove the duck from the oven and pour off any excess fat. Reduce the heat to 190°C (375°F), Gas Mark 5. Sprinkle the duck with the spring onions, any remaining marinade and the stock. Cover well with foil. Return to the oven and cook for 1 hour, basting occasionally.

Place the duck on a board, joint it and chop it into pieces. Transfer to a warmed serving dish; keep hot.

Put the pineapple and juice in a pan. Stir in the sherry, the blended cornflour and the duck juices. Cook for 2 minutes and serve in a sauce bowl. To serve, garnish with pineapple and spring onions.

Serves 4–6

Oriental Duck with Pineapple

The combination of simmering and frying makes the duck meat both tender and well flavoured. You can use canned pineapple in natural juice instead of the fresh fruit. Served with steamed or boiled rice, this dish makes a complete meal in itself.

2.4 kg (4½ lb) oven-ready duck
1.2 litres (2 pints) water
3 tablespoons dark soy sauce
1 fresh pineapple
250 g (8 oz) can water chestnuts
1 bunch of spring onions, sliced diagonally
2 green chillies
sesame oil, for greasing
1 large garlic clove

left: pleasure-boat duck
above: soy-braised duck

Cut the duck in half lengthways. Place the halves in a wok and pour in the water, then add 1 tablespoon of the soy sauce. Put the lid on the wok and bring to the boil. Reduce the heat so that the liquid simmers steadily and cook for 1 hour.

Meanwhile, prepare the remaining ingredients. Trim the leaves from the pineapple and cut off the stalk end. Cut off the peel and cut out all the spines, then slice the fruit in half lengthways and remove the hard core. Cut the pineapple halves into slices and set aside. Drain and slice the water chestnuts. Cut the stalks from the chillies and remove all the seeds, then slice the green part thinly.

Remove the duck from the stock and set it aside. Pour the stock out of the wok (this should be chilled and the fat skimmed off, then the stock could be used in soups and stews) and wipe out the pan. Grease it with a little sesame oil.

When the duck is cool enough to handle cut all the meat from the bones and slice it into pieces. Heat the wok and add the chillies, crush the garlic into the pan and add the duck. Stir-fry until lightly browned, then add the water chestnuts and pineapple and cook for a few minutes. Stir in the remaining soy sauce and any juice from the fruit, and sprinkle over the spring onions. Cook for 1 minute then serve hot, straight from the wok on a bed of rice, if you like.

Serves 4

Nanking Spiced Duck

125 g (4 oz) coarse salt
3 teaspoons Sichuan peppercorns
2 kg (4 lb) oven-ready duck
To garnish:
chilli flowers (optional)
cucumber twists and slices

Place the salt and peppercorns in a frying pan and dry-fry over a high heat for 10 minutes to brown, but not burn; set aside to cool.

Rub this mixture thoroughly over the inside and outside of the duck. Wrap it lightly in foil and store in the refrigerator for 3 days.

Remove the foil and place the duck on a rack in a roasting tin. Cook in a preheated moderately hot oven, 200°C (400°F), Gas Mark 6, for 1¼–1½ hours, until golden.

Transfer to a warmed serving dish and garnish with chilli flowers, if using, and cucumber. Serve immediately.

Serves 4–6

Wonton Duck

2 kg (4 lb) oven-ready duck
1.2 litres (2 pints) water
4–5 tablespoons soy sauce
4 slices fresh root ginger
Sauce:
1 red pepper, cored, deseeded and
    thinly sliced
1 carrot, cut into matchsticks
1 small onion, thinly sliced
1 tablespoon oil
2 tablespoons tomato ketchup
2 tablespoons cider vinegar
2 tablespoons dry sherry
1 tablespoon sugar
900 ml (1½ pints) oil, for deep-frying
16–20 ready-made wonton squares

Trim the ends of the wings and legs from the duck and cut it in half lengthways. Place the halves in a wok and pour in the water. Add 3 tablespoons of the soy sauce and the ginger and bring to the boil. Reduce the heat to a steady simmer and put the lid on the wok. Cook for 1 hour, topping up the water if necessary and turning the duck half-way through the cooking time.

To prepare the sauce, cut the stalk end from the red pepper and remove the seeds and pith from the inside, then halve and thinly slice the flesh. Cut the carrot into very fine strips and halve and thinly slice the onion, separating the pieces into fine strips.

When the duck is cooked, remove it from the wok and drain thoroughly. Leave until cool

enough to handle, then cut off all the meat. Discard any fat and cut the meat into strips. Pour off the stock, reserving it for use in soups and stews. Rinse and wipe out the wok, greasing it if necessary.

Add the oil to the wok and heat over a high heat. Fry the strips of duck until browned, then add the pepper, carrot and onion strips and cook quickly over a high heat. Stir in the ketchup, vinegar, sherry, the remaining soy sauce and the sugar and bring to the boil. Transfer to a dish and keep hot.

To cook the wontons, wipe the wok and add the oil for deep-frying. Heat to 190°C (375°F) then add the squares of wonton dough, a few at a time, and cook them until crisp and golden brown. Place them on a heated serving platter and spoon the duck with its sauce into the centre. Serve immediately.

Serves 4

Peking Duck

2 kg (4 lb) oven-ready duck
2 tablespoons soy sauce
2 tablespoons dark brown sugar
Mandarin Pancakes:
500 g (1 lb) plain flour
pinch of salt
about 300 ml (½ pint) boiling water
sesame seed oil
To serve:
1 small cucumber, cut into 5 cm
  (2 inch) matchsticks

1 bunch spring onions, cut into 5 cm
  (2 inch) matchsticks
8 tablespoons hoisin sauce
spring onion flower

Immerse the duck in a pan of boiling water for 2 minutes, then drain it thoroughly. Hang the duck up in a well ventilated room and leave to dry overnight.

Mix together the soy sauce and sugar and rub it over the duck. Hang the duck for 2 hours until the coating is dry.

Place the duck on a rack in a roasting tin and cook in a preheated moderately hot oven, 200°C (400°F), Gas Mark 6, for 1½ hours.

Meanwhile, make the pancakes. Sift the flour and salt into a mixing bowl. Gradually add the boiling water, mixing to make a stiff dough. Knead and shape into a roll, 5 cm (2 inches) in diameter. Cut it into 2 cm (½ inch) slices, then roll out into thin 15 cm (6 inch) pancakes. Brush one side of each pancake with sesame seed oil and sandwich the pancakes together in pairs.

Place an ungreased frying pan over a high heat. When hot, lower the

heat slightly and place a pancake 'sandwich' in the pan. When it starts to puff up, turn and cook the other side until lightly browned.

Pull the pancakes apart and fold each one in half. Place on a warmed serving dish and cover with foil to prevent them from drying out.

Cut off all the crispy skin from the duck and arrange it on a warmed serving dish and garnish with the cucumber. Remove all the meat and arrange on another warmed dish. Garnish with the spring onion. Place the hoisin sauce in a bowl. Garnish the pancakes with a spring onion flower.

To eat, spread a little hoisin sauce over a pancake. Cover with a piece of duck skin and meat, then top with a few pieces of cucumber and spring onion. Roll up the pancake, tucking one end in to prevent the filling from spilling out.

Serves 4–6

left: nanking spiced duck
above: peking duck

Braised Duck

2.5 litres (4 pints) water

2.5 kg (5 lb) oven-ready duckling

3 spring onions

5 tablespoons soy sauce

3 tablespoons sherry

1 tablespoon brandy

3 tablespoons coffee sugar crystals

To garnish (optional):

pineapple slices

glacé cherries

parsley sprigs

Bring the water to boil in a large saucepan or casserole, put in the duck and boil rapidly for 4–5 minutes, turning it over once or twice. Discard two-thirds of the water, then add the spring onions, soy sauce, sherry and brandy.

Bring the water back to the boil, then cover tightly and simmer gently for 30 minutes, turning the duck over at least once. Add the sugar and continue cooking for a further 1–1½ hours.

Serve the duck whole in its juices and garnished with pineapple, glacé cherries and a sprig of parsley, or cut the duck into small pieces and arrange them neatly on a plate. Serve hot with rice or noodles as an accompaniment, or cold with a bean sprout salad.

Serves 4

top right: braised duck
right: duck with almonds

Duck with Almonds

500 g (1 lb) lean duck meat

2 slices fresh root ginger, peeled and shredded

1 garlic clove, crushed

3 tablespoons oil

3–4 dried Chinese mushrooms (optional)

4 spring onions, sliced

125 g (4 oz) canned bamboo shoots, drained and sliced

3 tablespoons soy sauce

2 tablespoons dry sherry

2 teaspoons cornflour, blended with 1 tablespoon water

25 g (1 oz) flaked almonds, toasted

Cut the duck into small pieces and place in a bowl with the ginger and garlic. Pour over 1 tablespoon of oil. Cover and marinate for 30 minutes.

Soak the mushrooms, if using, in warm water for 15 minutes. Squeeze dry, discard the hard stalks, then slice the mushroom caps.

Heat the remaining oil in a wok or frying pan, add the spring onions and stir-fry for 30 seconds. Add the duck and cook for 2 minutes. Add the mushrooms, bamboo shoots, soy sauce and sherry and cook for 2 minutes. Stir in the blended cornflour. Cook for 1 minute, stirring, until thickened. Stir in the toasted almonds and serve.

Serves 4–6

Chicken Wings with Oyster Sauce

500 g (1 lb) chicken wings
4 spring onions, chopped
2.5 cm (1 inch) piece fresh root ginger, peeled and shredded
1 garlic clove, sliced
1 tablespoon soy sauce
2 tablespoons dry sherry
2 tablespoons oil
2 leeks, sliced
3 tablespoons oyster sauce
To garnish (optional):
radish flowers
cucumber slices

Trim the tips from the chicken wings, then cut the wings in half at the joints.

Put the spring onions, ginger, garlic, soy sauce and sherry in a bowl. Add the chicken wings and stir well to coat, then cover and leave to marinate for 15 minutes.

Heat the oil in a wok or deep frying pan, add the chicken and the marinade and stir-fry gently for 15 minutes. Add the leeks and oyster sauce and cook for a further 3–4 minutes.

Transfer to a warmed serving dish and serve immediately, garnished with radish flowers and cucumber slices, if you like.

Serves 4–6

Deep-fried Chicken Legs

2 tablespoons dry sherry
2 tablespoons soy sauce
1 teaspoon sugar
2.5 cm (1 inch) piece root ginger, finely chopped
2 garlic cloves, crushed
8 chicken drumsticks
50 g (2 oz) plain flour
1–2 eggs, beaten
oil, for deep-frying
To garnish:
radish flowers, placed inside of green chilli flowers
cucumber slices

Put the sherry, soy sauce, sugar, ginger and garlic into a bowl and mix well. Add the drumsticks, turn to coat, cover and leave to marinate for 1 hour. Remove the chicken and reserve the marinade.

Put the flour into a bowl, beat in the eggs, then mix in the marinade, stirring well to form a smooth paste. Coat the chicken in the mixture.

Heat the oil in a wok or deep-fryer and deep-fry the chicken legs for 12–15 minutes until golden brown. Drain on kitchen paper.

Garnish with the radish and chilli flowers and cucumber slices.

Serves 4–6

top left: chicken wings with oyster sauce; **left:** *deep-fried chicken legs*

Diced Chicken with Peppers

This is a very colourful dish with a piquant flavour and delightful texture. The meat should be tender and the peppers crisp and crunchy.

250 g (8 oz) boneless, skinless chicken breast meat
½ teaspoon salt
1 egg white
1 tablespoon cornflour
1 green pepper, cored and deseeded
1 red pepper, cored and deseeded
2 slices fresh ginger root, peeled
2 spring onions
2 chillies, deseeded
4 tablespoons oil
2 tablespoons crushed black bean sauce

Dice the chicken meat into small cubes. Mix the cubes with first the salt, then the egg white and finally the cornflour. It is very important that the ingredients are mixed in this order.

Cut the green and red peppers into small square pieces about the same size as the chicken cubes. Then cut the ginger, spring onions and chillies into slivers.

Heat the oil in a wok or frying pan and stir-fry the chicken over a moderate heat, separating the cubes. Cook until the cubes are lightly coloured, then remove them with a slotted spoon. Drain the chicken on kitchen paper and keep warm until needed.

Increase the heat and when the oil is really hot, add the ginger, spring onions and chillies, stir a few times then add the green and red peppers. Continue stirring for about 30 seconds, then add the black bean sauce and the reserved chicken cubes, stirring constantly for about 1–1½ minutes. Serve immediately, accompanied by small bowls of boiled white rice, if you like.

Serves 4

below: diced chicken with peppers;
top right: chicken salad;
bottom right: braised chicken with peppers and corn

Chicken Salad

Chilli sauce is very hot, so use it cautiously according to your taste.

500 g (1 lb) cooked chicken meat
1 small cucumber
50 g (2 oz) fresh root ginger, peeled
4 spring onions (white parts only)
Dressing:
1½ teaspoons salt
1 tablespoon sugar
1 tablespoon lemon juice
1–2 teaspoons chilli sauce
1 tablespoon sesame seed oil
finely chopped parsley, to garnish

Cut the chicken into fine shreds about the size of a matchstick. Cut the cucumber, ginger and spring onions into thin shreds. Place them with the chicken in a large bowl.

Mix together all the dressing ingredients and pour over the chicken mixture. Toss the salad well then cover and allow the flavours to blend for 1 hour before serving.

Serves 4

Braised Chicken with Peppers and Corn

1 tablespoon oil

3 spring onions, chopped

2 x 2.5 cm (1 inch) pieces fresh root ginger, peeled and shredded

500 g (1 lb) boneless, skinless chicken breast, shredded

2 tablespoons light soy sauce

2 tablespoons dry sherry

2 green peppers, cored, deseeded and sliced

425 g (14 oz) can baby corn or sweetcorn, drained

Heat the oil in a wok or frying pan, add the spring onions and ginger and fry for 1 minute. Add the chicken and brown lightly. Pour in the soy sauce and sherry and cook for 1 minute more. Add the peppers and corn and stir-fry for 2 minutes.

Pile the mixture on to a warmed serving dish and serve immediately.

Serves 4–6

Diced Chicken with Chillies

2 tablespoons oil

1 garlic clove, sliced

375 g (12 oz) boneless, skinless chicken breast, diced

1 red pepper, cored, deseeded and diced

2 green chillies, deseeded and thinly sliced

50 g (2 oz) bean sprouts

2 tablespoons soy sauce

2 tablespoons chilli sauce

coriander leaves, to garnish

Heat the oil in a wok or deep frying pan, add the garlic and fry quickly for 1 minute. Add the chicken and stir-fry for 1 minute. Add the red pepper and chillies and cook for a further minute. Stir in the bean sprouts, soy sauce and chilli sauce and cook for 2 minutes.

Turn into a warmed serving dish, garnish with coriander and serve.

Serves 4

Sesame Chicken

500 g (1 lb) boneless, skinless chicken breast

1 tablespoon oil

125 g (4 oz) unsalted cashew nuts

75 g (3 oz) straw mushrooms, halved

Marinade:

3 spring onions, chopped

3 tablespoons soy sauce

2 tablespoons hot pepper oil

2 tablespoons sesame seed oil

1 tablespoon sesame seed paste

1 teaspoon ground Sichuan peppercorns

Put all the marinade ingredients into a bowl. Cut the chicken into cubes, then add it to the marinade, turning to coat well. Cover and leave to marinate for 30 minutes.

Heat the oil in a wok or frying pan, add the cashew nuts and fry, stirring occasionally until golden brown. Drain on kitchen paper.

Add the chicken and marinade to the pan and stir-fry for 2 minutes. Then add the mushrooms and cook for 1 minute more. Pile the mixture carefully on to a warmed serving dish and sprinkle with the reserved cashew nuts. Serve immediately.

Serves 4–6

above left: diced chicken with chillies;
above right: sesame chicken;
right: lemon chicken

Lemon Chicken

5–6 Chinese dried mushrooms

1.5–2 kg (3–4 lb) oven-ready chicken

5 tablespoons vegetable oil

15 g (½ oz) lard or butter

4 slices fresh root ginger, chopped

1 red pepper, cored, deseeded and
   shredded

shredded rind of 2 lemons

5 spring onions, thinly sliced

4 tablespoons dry sherry

1½ teaspoons sugar

2 tablespoons light soy sauce

1 teaspoon cornflour

1–2 tablespoons lemon juice

salt and pepper

lemon twists, to garnish

Soak the mushroom in warm water for 20 minutes. Squeeze dry and remove the hard stalks, then shred the mushroom caps.

Cut the chicken into bite-sized pieces and mix with the salt and pepper to taste and 1½ tablespoons of the oil. Heat the remaining oil in a wok or frying pan. Add the chicken and stir-fry for 2 minutes; remove and keep warm.

Add the lard or butter to the pan.

When the fat has melted, add the ginger, red pepper and mushrooms and stir-fry for 1 minute. Add the lemon rind and spring onions and stir-fry quickly for 30 seconds.

Sprinkle in the sherry, sugar and soy sauce and bring to the boil. Blend the cornflour with 1 tablespoon of water and stir into the mixture. Return the chicken to the wok or pan and cook, stirring, for 1 minute. Sprinkle with lemon juice and serve hot, garnished with lemon slices.

Serves 6–8

Ginger Chicken

750 g (1½ lb) boneless, skinless chicken breasts, cut into small pieces
1 teaspoon sugar
4 tablespoons sesame oil
7.5–10 cm (3–4 inch) piece of fresh root ginger, peeled and finely sliced
75–120 ml (3–4 fl oz) water
125 g (4 oz) button mushrooms
2 tablespoons brandy
2 teaspoons cornflour, blended with 3 tablespoons water
1 teaspoon soy sauce
salt and pepper
coriander leaves, to garnish

Sprinkle the chicken with sugar and leave to stand for 20–30 minutes; this helps to release the juices. Season to taste with salt and pepper.

Heat the oil in a wok and fry the ginger slices. Add the chicken pieces and cook for 3 minutes. Stir in the water and mushrooms. Cover and cook for a further 5 minutes, or until the chicken is tender.

Add the brandy, blended cornflour and soy sauce. Bring to the boil, stirring constantly until the sauce thickens, then taste and adjust the seasoning. Arrange on a warmed serving plate and garnish with the coriander leaves.

Serves 4

right: soy chicken

Soy Chicken

2 tablespoons crushed yellow bean sauce
½ teaspoon five-spice powder
2 tablespoons water
1.5–1.75 kg (3–3½ lb) oven-ready chicken
2 slices fresh root ginger
2 spring onions, chopped
4 tablespoons soy sauce
2 tablespoons dry sherry
450 ml (¾ pint) chicken stock
shredded spring onion, to garnish
To serve:
lettuce leaves
radish flower (optional)

Mix the crushed bean sauce and five-spice powder with the water, then pour the mixture into the cavity of the chicken.

Place the chicken in a saucepan or flameproof casserole dish and add the ginger, spring onions, soy sauce, sherry and stock. Simmer gently for about 1½ hours, turning the chicken several times during cooking and basting it frequently with the sauce.

Remove the chicken from the pan and leave to cool. Cut the chicken into pieces and serve on a bed of lettuce with radish flowers, if using, and garnished with the spring onion and accompanied with a Celery Salad (see pages 84–5).

Serves 4

Drunken Chicken

1.5 kg (3–3½ lb) oven-ready chicken
2 teaspoons salt
2 pieces of fresh root ginger, peeled and sliced
4 spring onions
1.8 litres (3 pints) water
finely chopped parsley, to garnish
Sauce:
2 tablespoons soy sauce
1 tablespoon brown sugar
300 ml (½ pint) dry sherry
1 tablespoon brandy

Rub the chicken with a little of the salt then leave it to stand for about 20 minutes. Place the remaining salt, ginger, spring onions and water in a saucepan or flameproof casserole and bring to the boil. Add the chicken, cover and bring to the boil, then reduce the heat and cook for 15 minutes. Bring the water to a rapid boil, then turn off the heat and leave the chicken to cool in the water for at least 2–3 hours before taking it out.

Cut the chicken into small pieces, arrange it neatly in a deep dish with the skin-side underneath. Place all the sauce ingredients in a pan and bring to the boil, stirring to dissolve the sugar. Immediately pour the sauce over the chicken then cover and chill in the refrigerator for about 2–3 hours.

Serve the chilled chicken skin-side up, sprinkled with parsley.

Serves 4

Chicken and Bean Sprouts

250 g (8 oz) boneless, skinless chicken breast
2 teaspoons salt
1 egg white
1 tablespoon cornflour
4 tablespoons oil
250 g (8 oz) fresh bean sprouts
1 small red pepper, cored, deseeded and cut into thin shreds
2 tablespoons chicken or vegetable stock

Slice the chicken meat into slivers not much bigger than a matchstick. Mix the slivers with ½ teaspoon of the salt, then the egg white and finally the cornflour.

Heat the oil in a wok or frying pan and stir-fry the chicken pieces until lightly coloured, then remove them with a slotted spoon.

Increase the heat and when the oil is hot, add the bean sprouts and red pepper followed by the chicken. Stir a few times, then add the remaining salt and the stock. Cook for about 1 minute more. Serve hot or cold.

Serves 4

*above left: drunken chicken; **above right**: chicken and bean sprouts*

Chilli Chicken

750 g (1½ lb) boneless, skinless
  chicken breasts
1 teaspoon sugar
3–6 fresh red chillies, deseeded
2 macadamia nuts or 4 almonds
1 stem lemon grass, trimmed and
  sliced
1 teaspoon fenugreek
2.5 cm (1 inch) piece fresh root
  ginger, peeled
6 small red onions or shallots, sliced
4 garlic cloves, crushed
4 tablespoons oil
150 ml (¼ pint) water
salt
shredded spring onion, to garnish

Cut each chicken breast lengthways
into pieces and sprinkle with sugar.

Pound the chillies with the nuts,
lemon grass, fenugreek and half of
the ginger using a pestle and mortar
or blend in a food processor.
Transfer to a small bowl. Pound or
blend the remaining ginger with the
onions and garlic in the same way
and transfer to a second bowl.

Heat the oil in a wok and fry the
spice mixture for 1–2 minutes. Add
the onion mixture and fry for a
further 1–2 minutes, stirring well.

Add the chicken, turning in the
sauce until well coated. Add the
water and salt to taste. Cover and
cook gently for 5 minutes. Transfer
to a warmed serving dish and
garnish with spring onion.

Serves 4

Shredded
Chicken and
Celery

Although the chicken is simmered for
only 15 minutes, it continues to cook in
the hot water until deliciously tender.

250 g (8 oz) boneless, skinless chicken
  breast
½ teaspoon salt
1 egg white
1 tablespoon cornflour
1 small celery stick
1 green pepper, cored and deseeded
4 slices fresh root ginger, peeled
2 spring onions
4 tablespoons oil
2 tablespoons soy sauce
1 tablespoon dry sherry
cucumber slices, to garnish

Cut the chicken meat into fine
slivers. Mix them first with the salt,
then the egg white and then the
cornflour. Cut the celery, reserving
some leaves, green pepper, ginger
and spring onions into slivers.

Heat the oil in a wok or frying
pan and stir-fry the chicken shreds
over a moderate heat until the
pieces are lightly coloured. Remove
the chicken with a slotted spoon.

Increase the heat, and when the
oil is very hot, add the ginger and
spring onions followed by the celery
and green pepper. Stir continuously
for about 30 seconds, then return
the chicken to the wok or pan with
the soy sauce and sherry. Blend well
and cook for 1 further minute,
stirring constantly. Serve hot,
garnished with cucumber slices and
the reserved celery leaves.

Serves 4

Sichuan Bang Bang Chicken

This popular dish is extremely simple to cook. If you cannot get sesame sauce (sometimes called sesame paste), an acceptable substitute is peanut butter creamed with a little sesame seed oil.

175 g (6 oz) boneless, skinless chicken breast
1 lettuce heart
Sauce:
1 tablespoon sesame sauce
1 tablespoon light soy sauce
2 teaspoons vinegar
1 teaspoon chilli sauce
1 teaspoon sugar
2 tablespoons chicken stock

Put the chicken meat in a saucepan and cover with cold water. Bring to the boil, then reduce the heat and simmer gently for 10 minutes. Remove the chicken and beat it with a rolling pin until soft (hence the name of the dish).

Cut the lettuce leaves into shreds and place them in a serving dish. Pull the chicken into shreds with your fingers and place it on top of the lettuce leaves.

Mix together all the ingredients for the sauce and pour the sauce evenly over the chicken. Serve cold.

Serves 2

left: shredded chicken and celery;
right: sichuan bang bang chicken

Sichuan-style Chicken with Walnuts

The walnuts can be replaced by the same quantity of almonds, cashew nuts or peanuts.

250 g–300 g (8–10 oz) boneless, skinless chicken

½ teaspoon salt

1 egg white

1 tablespoon cornflour

1 green pepper, cored and deseeded

50 g (2 oz) walnuts, shelled

4 tablespoons oil

2 spring onions, finely chopped

2 slices fresh root ginger, peeled and finely chopped

Sauce:

1 tablespoon crushed yellow bean sauce

2 teaspoons sugar

2 tablespoons rice wine or dry sherry

1 tablespoon chilli sauce

2 teaspoons cornflour, blended with 1 tablespoon water

Cut the chicken meat into small cubes about the size of sugar lumps. Mix with first the salt, then the egg white and finally the cornflour.

Cut the green peppers and walnuts into pieces the same size as the chicken cubes.

Heat the oil in a preheated wok or frying pan, stir-fry the chicken cubes for 10 seconds, then remove with a slotted spoon.

Add the spring onions, ginger and walnuts to the hot oil, followed by the yellow bean sauce. Stir a few times, then add the green peppers, and chicken cubes. Stir a few times more, then add the sugar, wine or sherry and chilli sauce and cook for 30 seconds. Finally, add the cornflour and water mixture, blend well and serve hot.

Serves 4

Chicken Spring Rolls

Serve these tasty spring rolls as an appetizer with dipping bowls of chilli sauce and sweet and sour sauce, or as a main course accompanied by a green salad with the sauces served separately.

Cooked spring rolls can be frozen, then reheated in a preheated oven 180°C (350°F), Gas Mark 4.

Filling:

50 g (2 oz) cellophane noodles, soaked in water for 10 minutes

2 tablespoons dried Chinese mushrooms, soaked in warm water for 30 minutes

500 g (1 lb) boneless, skinless chicken breasts, cut into thin strips

3 garlic cloves, finely chopped

3 shallots, finely chopped

250 g (8 oz) crab meat, canned or frozen

½ teaspoon black pepper

450 ml (¾ pint) oil, for deep frying

shredded spring onion, to garnish

Wrappers:

4 eggs, beaten

20 dried rice papers

Drain the cellophane noodles, then cut them into 2.5 cm (1 inch) pieces. Finely chop the mushrooms.

To make the filling, put all the ingredients in a large bowl and mix well by hand. Divide the mixture into about 20 portions and shape them into small cylinders.

To assemble each spring roll, brush beaten egg over the entire surface of each piece of rice paper. Leave for a few seconds until soft and flexible. Place the prepared filling along the curved edge of the paper, roll once, then fold over the sides to enclose the filling and continue rolling. (The beaten egg holds the wrapper together.)

Heat the oil in a wok and deep-fry about one-third of the spring rolls over a moderate heat until golden brown. Remove with a slotted spoon and drain on kitchen paper. Fry the remaining spring rolls in the same way. Serve hot or warm, garnished with spring onion.

Makes about 20 rolls

*left: sichuan-style chicken with walnuts; **below:** shredded chicken with green peppers*

Shredded Chicken with Green Peppers

The purpose of marinating chicken breast meat with salt, egg-white and cornflour before cooking is a technique known as velveting. The coating forms an impenetrable barrier between the meat and the hot oil, thus preserving the delicate texture of the chicken breast. Another point to remember here is that the oil should not be too hot, nor the heat too high when cooking the chicken meat for the first stage.

2 boneless, skinless chicken breasts
1½ teaspoons salt
1 egg white
3 teaspoons cornflour
250 g (8 oz) green peppers, cored and deseeded
1 spring onion, finely chopped
2 slices fresh root ginger, peeled and finely chopped
4 tablespoons oil
2 tablespoons rice wine or dry sherry
1 teaspoon sesame seed oil, to garnish

Remove the white tendon and membrane from the chicken breast meat, then cut the meat into matchstick shreds. Mix the shreds of chicken with ½ teaspoon of the salt, then with the egg white and 2 teaspoons of the cornflour.

Thinly shred the green pepper into pieces about the same size as the chicken shreds.

Heat the oil in a preheated wok or frying pan, stir-fry the chicken shreds over a moderate heat, turning frequently, until their colour changes to white, then remove them with a slotted spoon and drain on kitchen paper.

Increase the heat to high and when the oil is very hot, add the spring onion and ginger to flavour the oil. Add the green peppers, stir continuously for about 30 seconds, then add the chicken shreds with the remaining salt and the wine or sherry. Stir for a further 30 seconds or so, then add the remaining cornflour mixed with a little water. Blend well, then add the sesame seed oil as a garnish. Serve hot.

Serves 2–3

Chicken with Celery

2 boneless, skinless large chicken breasts
½ teaspoon salt
1 egg white
1 tablespoon cornflour
1 small head celery
4 tablespoons oil
1 tablespoon rice wine or dry sherry
1 tablespoon light soy sauce

Dice the chicken into small cubes about the size of sugar lumps. Mix with the salt, then the egg white and about ½ tablespoon of the cornflour.

Cut the celery into small chunks diagonally, roughly the same size as the chicken cubes.

Warm the oil in a preheated wok or frying pan. Stir-fry the chicken cubes over a moderate heat for 30 seconds or until their colour turns to white, then scoop them out with a slotted spoon.

Increase the heat and when the oil is very hot, stir-fry the celery for about 1 minute, then add the chicken with the wine or sherry and soy sauce and cook for 1 further minute only. Finally, add the remaining cornflour mixed with a little water, blend well and serve hot. The chicken should be tender and the celery crisp and crunchy.

Serves 3–4

Boiled Noodles with Chicken and Mushrooms

325 g (11 oz) egg noodles
8 Chinese dried mushrooms or 250 g (8 oz) fresh mushrooms
200 g (7 oz) boneless, skinless chicken breast
2 teaspoons cornflour
1 litre (1¾ pints) chicken stock
8 tablespoons oil
250 g (8 oz) bamboo shoots, cut into thin strips
250 g (8 oz) spinach leaves, cut into thin strips
4 spring onions, finely chopped
2 slices fresh root ginger, peeled and finely chopped
Sauce:
8 tablespoons soy sauce
4 tablespoons sherry
2 teaspoons salt
2 teaspoons sugar

Bring a saucepan of water to the boil, add the noodles and simmer for 5 minutes until soft but not sticky. Drain them through a sieve and place in a large warmed bowl and keep warm.

Soak the Chinese dried mushrooms in warm water for about 20 minutes, then squeeze dry and discard the hard stalks. Cut the mushrooms into thin pieces.

Cut the chicken into thin pieces and mix with the cornflour, tossing to cover the pieces thoroughly.

Bring the chicken stock to the boil and then pour it over the cooked noodles.

Heat the oil in a wok or frying pan and add the chicken, followed by the bamboo shoots, mushrooms, spinach leaves, spring onions, and ginger, in that order. Stir-fry the mixture for about 1 minute. Mix together all the sauce ingredients and pour the sauce into the wok or pan. Cook stirring well for another 1–2 minutes. Pour the chicken and vegetables over the noodles and serve immediately.

Serves 3–4

*above: boiled noodles with chicken and mushrooms; **left:** chicken with celery*

Chicken with Chestnuts

Fresh cooked chestnuts may be used in place of soaked dried ones.

125 g (4 oz) dried chestnuts
500 g (1 lb) boneless, skinless chicken
  breast
½ teaspoon salt
2 tablespoons oil
2 garlic cloves, sliced
2.5 cm (1 inch) piece fresh root
  ginger, peeled and finely chopped
4 spring onions, each cut into
  4 pieces
2 tablespoons soy sauce
2 tablespoons dry sherry
2 teaspoons sugar
1 tablespoon cornflour, blended with
  2 tablespoons water

Soak the chestnuts in warm water for 1 hour. Drain well and set aside. Cut the chicken into cubes and toss to cover in the salt.

Heat the oil in a wok or deep frying pan, add the garlic and fry until browned. Add the ginger, spring onions and chicken and stir-fry for 1 minute. Add the chestnuts and cook for 2 minutes. Add the soy sauce, sherry and sugar.

Stir the blended cornflour into the pan and cook, stirring, for about 1 minute.

Spoon into a warmed serving dish and serve immediately.

Serves 4–6

Chicken with Peppers and Cashew Nuts

3 tablespoons dry sherry
1 egg white
1 teaspoon cornflour
2 boneless, skinless chicken breasts,
  cut into small pieces
2 tablespoons oil
2 spring onions, chopped
1 green pepper, cored, deseeded and
  diced
125 g (4 oz) canned bamboo shoots,
  drained and shredded
1 tablespoon soy sauce
125 g (4 oz) unsalted cashew nuts

Mix 2 tablespoons of the sherry with the egg white and cornflour in a large bowl. Add the chicken and toss well until evenly coated.

Heat the oil in a wok or frying pan, add the spring onions and stir-fry for 30 seconds. Add the chicken and cook for 3 minutes. Then add the green pepper, bamboo shoots, soy sauce and cashew nuts and cook for 2 minutes.

Pile into a warmed serving dish and serve immediately.

Serves 4

Chicken in Foil

1 tablespoon soy sauce
1 tablespoon dry sherry
1 tablespoon sesame seed oil, plus
  extra for brushing
500 g (1 lb) boneless, skinless chicken
  breast, cut into 16 equal pieces
4 spring onions, each cut into
  4 pieces
2 x 2.5 cm (1 inch) pieces fresh root
  ginger, peeled and shredded
1 celery stick, shredded

Mix the soy sauce, sherry and sesame seed oil in a large bowl. Add the chicken and toss well to coat, then cover and leave to marinate for 15–20 minutes.

Cut out 16 pieces of foil large enough to enclose the pieces of chicken generously. Brush each piece of foil with oil, place a piece of chicken in the centre and top with a piece of spring onion, some ginger and celery. Fold the foil over to enclose the chicken and seal the edges well. Place in a steamer and steam for 10–12 minutes.

Serve hot still wrapped in the foil so when the foil is opened, the fragrant aroma is released.

Serves 4

*near right: chicken with chestnuts,
far right: chicken with cashew nuts;
bottom right: chicken in foil*

Pork

Pork Spare Ribs in Cantonese Sweet and Sour Sauce

500 g (1 lb) pork spare ribs

½ teaspoon salt

freshly ground Sichuan or black
  pepper

1 teaspoon sugar

1 egg yolk

1 tablespoon cornflour

oil, for deep-frying

2 tablespoons plain flour

1 small green pepper, cored,
  deseeded and thinly sliced

1 small red pepper, cored, deseeded
  and thinly sliced

Sauce:

1 tablespoon soy sauce

3 tablespoons sugar

3 tablespoons vinegar

1 tablespoon cornflour, blended with
  3 tablespoons water

To garnish:

finely sliced green chilli flower

tomato flower

Chop each spare rib into 2–3 pieces. Place them in a bowl and add the salt, pepper, sugar, egg yolk and cornflour. Mix well and leave to marinate for about 10 minutes.

Heat the oil in a wok or deep saucepan until hot, then reduce the heat to low and let the oil cool a little. Coat each spare rib piece in plain flour before deep-frying them. Put them into the oil so that they do not stick together, separating them if necessary. Increase the heat to high after a few minutes and fry until crisp and golden, then remove with a slotted spoon.

Heat the oil until bubbling and fry the spare ribs once more for about 30 seconds, or until golden brown. Remove with a slotted spoon and drain.

Pour off most of the oil, leaving about 1 tablespoon in the wok and stir-fry the green and red peppers for a few seconds. Add the soy sauce, sugar and vinegar. Stir a few times, then add the blended cornflour, stirring continuously. When the sauce becomes a smooth paste, return the spare ribs, mix well and serve immediately garnished with the chilli and tomato flowers.

Serves 4

Pork Slices with Chinese Vegetables

250 g (8 oz) pork fillet
1 tablespoon soy sauce
1 tablespoon rice wine or dry sherry
1 tablespoon cornflour
125 g (4 oz) bamboo shoots
15 g (½ oz) wood ears
125 g (4 oz) mangetout or broccoli
125 g (4 oz) water chestnuts
2 spring onions
4 tablespoons oil
1 teaspoon salt
1 teaspoon sugar
1 teaspoon sesame seed oil

Cut the pork into thin slices about the size of large postage stamps, then mix it with the soy sauce, wine or sherry and ½ tablespoon of the cornflour.

Cut the bamboo shoots into pieces roughly the same size as the pork. Soak the wood ears in warm water for 10–15 minutes. Rinse in fresh water and discard the hard stalks, then cut them into small pieces. Top and tail the mangetout and leave whole if they are small otherwise snap them in half. If using broccoli, cut it into small pieces. Cut the water chestnuts into 2–3 pieces and cut the spring onions into short lengths.

Heat the oil in a preheated wok or frying pan, and stir-fry the pork over a high heat for about 1 minute or until the colour changes. Lift out with a slotted spoon and set aside.

In the remaining hot oil, stir-fry the spring onions, followed by the mangetout or broccoli. (As broccoli takes longer to cook, allow an extra minute or so before adding the remaining ingredients.) Add the bamboo shoots, mushrooms and water chestnuts. Add the salt and sugar, stir a few more times, then add the pork, stirring for about 1 minute, followed by the remaining cornflour blended with a little water and mix well until thickened. Finally, add the sesame seed oil and serve hot.

Serves 4

Stir-fried Pork with Mushrooms and Bamboo Shoots

4 Chinese dried mushrooms
250 g (8 oz) pork fillet
2 tablespoons soy sauce
1 tablespoon cornflour
250 g (8 oz) bamboo shoots
4 tablespoons oil
1½ teaspoons salt
2 tablespoons dry sherry

Soak the mushrooms in warm water for about 20 minutes, then squeeze dry and discard the hard stalks. Halve or quarter the mushrooms depending on their size. Retain the soaking liquid.

Cut the pork into thin slices about the size of a large postage stamp. Mix together the soy sauce and cornflour in a bowl, then add the pork and mix well to coat the pork thoroughly.

Cut the bamboo shoots into thin slices about the same size as the pieces of pork.

Heat about half the oil in a wok or frying pan and stir-fry the pork slices for about 1 minute or until lightly coloured. Remove the pork with a slotted spoon and set aside.

Heat the remaining oil, stir-fry the mushrooms and bamboo shoots, then add the salt, pork and sherry, stirring well. Cook for a further minute or so, stirring constantly and, if necessary, add a little of the mushroom soaking liquid. Serve hot.

Serves 4

*far left: pork slices with chinese vegetables; **left**: pork spare ribs in cantonese sweet and sour sauce*

Red-cooked Pork

1 kg (2 lb) pork cut into cubes
1 garlic clove, crushed
4 tablespoons soy sauce
3 tablespoons sherry
50 g (2 oz) coffee sugar crystals
1 teaspoon five-spice powder
To garnish:
shredded spring onion
radish flower

Place the pork cubes in a saucepan or with enough water to cover. Add the garlic, soy sauce, sherry, sugar and five-spice powder and bring to the boil over a high heat. Reduce the heat, cover the pan and simmer gently for 1–1½ hours.

Serve hot with rice, garnished with spring onion and a radish.

Serves 4

Double-stir-fried Pork in Soy Bean Paste

750 g (1½ lb) lean pork
3 tablespoons vegetable oil
1 tablespoon hoisin sauce
1 tablespoon dry sherry
1½ teaspoons soy bean paste
1 tablespoon soy sauce
1 teaspoon sugar
15 g (½ oz) lard
1 teaspoon cornflour, blended with 3 tablespoons chicken stock or water
shredded lettuce or boiled white rice, to serve (optional)

Cut the pork into 2 cm (¾ inch) cubes. Place the cubes in a large bowl with 1½ tablespoons of the oil and turn to coat well.

In another bowl mix together the hoisin sauce, sherry, soy bean paste, soy sauce and sugar.

Heat the remaining oil in a wok or frying pan over high heat. Add the pork and stir-fry for 2 minutes, stirring occasionally. Remove with a slotted spoon, drain on kitchen paper and set aside. Discard the cooking oil from the pan.

Melt the lard in the wok, add the soy bean paste mixture and stir to combine well. Add the blended cornflour and cook, stirring, until thickened. Return the pork cubes to the pan and stir-fry for 1 minute.

Serve the pork hot on a bed of shredded lettuce or boiled white rice, if liked.

Serves 6

Pork and Cucumber

250 g (8 oz) pork fillet
1 tablespoon dry sherry
1 teaspoon cornflour
½ cucumber
3 tablespoons oil
1 teaspoon salt
1 teaspoon sugar
1 tablespoon soy sauce
1 tablespoon sesame seed oil

Cut the pork into thin slices about the size of a large postage stamp. Place the pork in a large bowl and mix with the sherry and cornflour.

Cut the cucumber into thin slices about the same size as the pork.

Heat the oil in a wok or frying pan and stir-fry the cucumber slices, reserving a few slices, for 1 minute. Add the pork followed by the salt, sugar and soy sauce and stir-fry for 2–3 minutes. Finally, add the sesame seed oil, blend well and serve immediately, garnished with the reserved cucumber slices.

Serves 4

above left: red-cooked pork
above right: pork and cucumber

Pork with Sichuan Preserved Vegetable

This is a traditional Sichuan dish that is also known as Twice-cooked Pork. Sichuan-style usually means the dish has a fairly hot taste, so if you prefer less hot food, either reduce the amount of Sichuan preserved vegetable, or use sweet bean paste instead of chilli bean paste. Before using the preserved vegetable, rinse off the paste in cold water and clean well. It will become a crunchy pickled vegetable with a salty aftertaste. Unused knobs of preserved vegetable should be stored unwashed in an airtight jar, in a cool place or in the refrigerator. It should then keep well indefinitely for future use.

250 g–300 g (8–10 oz) pork in one
   piece, not too lean
125 g (4 oz) Sichuan preserved
   vegetable, or to taste
125 g (4 oz) leeks, green pepper
   or broccoli
3 tablespoons oil
2 spring onions, finely chopped
2 slices fresh root ginger, peeled and
   finely chopped
1 garlic clove, finely chopped
1 tablespoon rice wine or dry sherry
1 tablespoon chilli bean paste or
   sweet bean paste
1 teaspoon cornflour, blended with
   1 tablespoon water

Place the whole piece of pork in a pan of boiling water and cook for 20–25 minutes. Remove the pork and let it cool a little before cutting it into thin slices about the size of a large postage stamp.

Cut the Sichuan preserved vegetable and leeks or other greens into slices about the same size as the pork.

Heat the oil in a preheated wok or deep frying pan and stir-fry the preserved vegetable and greens for about 1 minute, then add the pork, spring onions, ginger, garlic, wine or sherry and bean paste. Stir for 1 more minute, then add the blended cornflour and mix well. Serve hot.

Serves 4

Mu-shu Pork Shandong Style

Mu-shu is the Chinese name for cassia, a fragrant yellow flower that blooms in early autumn. Egg dishes in China are often given the name Mu-shu because of their bright yellow colour. Traditionally this dish is served as a filling wrapped in thin pancakes for a main course, but it can also be served on its own with rice or as a hot starter.

175 g–250 g (6–8 oz) pork steak
15 g (¼ oz) wood ears
250 g (8 oz) hard white cabbage
2 spring onions
3 eggs
1 teaspoon salt
4 tablespoons oil
1 tablespoon light soy sauce
1 tablespoon rice wine or dry sherry

Shred the pork into matchstick shreds. Soak the wood ears in water for about 20 minutes, then rinse well and thinly shred them. Cut the cabbage finely into thin shreds. Cut the spring onions into short pieces.

Lightly beat the eggs with a pinch of the salt. Heat 1 tablespoon of the oil in a wok or frying pan and scramble the eggs, until lightly set.

Heat the remaining oil and stir-fry the pork shreds for 30 seconds. Add the cabbage, wood ears and spring onions, stirring a few times, then add the remaining salt, soy sauce and wine or sherry. Continue stirring for 1–1½ minutes, finally add the scrambled eggs, stirring to break the eggs into shreds. When all the ingredients are well blended together, serve at once.

Serves 4

Variation: The cabbage can be substituted with bamboo shoots, celery or bean sprouts (do not use tinned bean sprouts, which will not have the crispness of fresh sprouts, the main characteristic of this very popular vegetable).

top right: pork with sichuan preserved vegetable; bottom right: mu-shu pork shandong style

Shredded Pork in Peking Bean Sauce

500 g (1 lb) leg of pork, boned but not skinned
450 ml (¾ pint) chicken stock
½ teaspoon salt
1 tablespoon crushed yellow bean sauce
2 tablespoons rice wine or dry sherry
2 tablespoons plain flour
1 small green pepper, cored and deseeded
oil, for deep-frying
1 teaspoon sugar
1 tablespoon soy sauce

Place the pork in a saucepan with the stock, bring to the boil. Cover and simmer for 25–30 minutes.

Take the pork out of the pan and remove the skin and cut into thin strips. Mix the salt, yellow bean sauce, wine or sherry and flour in a bowl, mix in the pork and marinate for about 10 minutes.

Cut the green pepper into strips the same size as the pork.

Heat the oil in a wok or saucepan until very hot. Fry the pork strips until golden, lift out with a slotted spoon and drain on kitchen paper.

Pour off the oil and return the pork to the pan. Add the sugar, soy sauce and green pepper, stirring well, over a high heat. Serve hot.

Serves 4

Aubergine and Pork in Hot Sauce

175 g (6 oz) boned lean pork, shredded
2 spring onions, finely chopped
1 slice fresh root ginger, peeled and finely chopped
1 garlic clove, finely chopped
1 tablespoon soy sauce
2 teaspoons rice wine or dry sherry
1½ teaspoons cornflour
300 ml (½ pint) oil, for deep-frying
250 g (8 oz) aubergine, cut into diamond-shaped chunks
1 tablespoon chilli sauce
3 tablespoons chicken stock or water
chopped spring onion, to garnish

Put the pork into a bowl with the spring onions, ginger, garlic, soy sauce, wine and cornflour. Mix well, then marinate for 20 minutes.

Heat the oil in a wok to 180°C (350°F). Lower the heat, add the aubergine and deep-fry for about 1½ minutes. Remove with a slotted spoon and drain on kitchen paper.

Pour off all but 1 tablespoon of oil from the wok. Add the pork, stir-fry for about 1 minute, then add the aubergine and chilli sauce and cook for about 1½ minutes, then add the stock or water. Simmer until the liquid has almost evaporated. Serve hot, garnished with spring onion.

Serves 4

Shredded Pork with Bean Sprouts

375 g (12 oz) boned lean pork, shredded
2 tablespoons soy sauce
1 teaspoon dry sherry
2 teaspoons cornflour
3 tablespoons vegetable oil
2 spring onions, shredded
1 slice fresh root ginger, peeled and shredded
1 teaspoon salt
250 g (8 oz) bean sprouts, washed
50 g (2 oz) leeks, shredded

Put the pork into a bowl. Sprinkle with the soy sauce, sherry and cornflour. Mix well and leave to marinate for about 20 minutes.

Heat 1 tablespoon of the oil in a wok or frying pan. Add the spring onions and ginger, then the pork. Stir-fry until the pork is evenly browned, then remove it from the wok and drain on kitchen paper.

Heat the remaining oil in the wok. Add the salt, then the bean sprouts and leeks. Stir-fry for about 1 minute. Return the pork to the pan, stir well and cook for 1 more minute. Serve hot.

Serves 4–6

---

left: shredded pork in peking bean sauce

Barbecued Pork Spare Ribs

Hoisin sauce is available from large supermarkets and Chinese food shops. However, you can make your own sauce quite simply as in this recipe.

750 g (1½ lb) pork spare ribs
2 tablespoons dry sherry
Hoisin sauce:
3 tablespoons crushed yellow bean sauce
1 tablespoon plain flour
1 tablespoon sugar
2 tablespoons vinegar
1 teaspoon chilli sauce
1 teaspoon sesame seed oil
1 garlic clove, crushed

First make the hoisin sauce. Put all the ingredients into a bowl and stir to mix. Chop the spare ribs roughly into small pieces. Marinate them in 4 tablespoons hoisin sauce and the sherry for at least 1 hour, turning over once or twice.

Cook the ribs on a barbecue griddle for about 10 minutes, turning them once or twice. Alternatively place the ribs on a baking sheet in a preheated oven, 220°C (425°F), Gas Mark 7, and roast for about 15–20 minutes until golden brown.

Serve with Chinese Fried Rice (see page 88) and a vegetable dish.

Serves 4

below: barbecued pork spare ribs
right: sweet and sour deep-fried pork

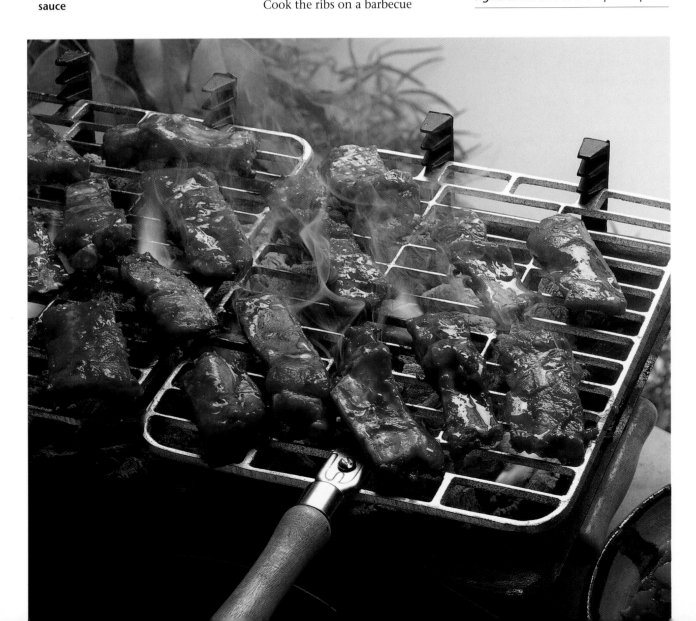

Braised Pork with Pumpkin

500 g (1 lb) pumpkin
375 g (12 oz) belly pork, skinned
2 tablespoons dry sherry
5 tablespoons soy sauce
3 tablespoons vegetable oil
300 ml (½ pint) chicken stock or
   water
2 teaspoons sugar

Peel the pumpkin, remove the seeds and cut it into 5 cm (2 inch) cubes. Cut the pork into 1 cm (½ inch) thick pieces.

Mix together half the sherry and 1 tablespoon of the soy sauce in a bowl. Add the pork and turn to coat thoroughly.

Heat the oil in a wok or frying pan, add the pork and stir-fry until evenly browned. Add the pumpkin.

Stir well, then add the stock or water, sugar and the remaining sherry and soy sauce. Bring to the boil and simmer gently for about 15 minutes, or until the pumpkin is tender. Serve hot.

Serves 4–6

Sweet and Sour Deep-fried Pork

250 g (8 oz) pork, not too lean
125 g (4 oz) bamboo shoots
1 green pepper, cored and deseeded
1 spring onion
1 teaspoon salt
1½ tablespoons brandy
1 egg, beaten
1 tablespoon cornflour
oil, for deep-frying
3 tablespoons plain flour

Sweet and Sour Sauce:
3 tablespoons vinegar
3 tablespoons sugar
½ teaspoon salt
1 tablespoon tomato purée
1 tablespoon soy sauce
1 tablespoon cornflour
1 teaspoon sesame seed oil

Cut the pork into about 24 small cubes. Cut the bamboo shoots and green pepper into small pieces of the same size. Then cut the spring onion into 2.5 cm (1 inch) lengths.

Mix the pork with the salt and brandy and marinate for 15 minutes. Add the beaten egg and the cornflour and blend well.

Mix together all the ingredients for the sauce.

Heat the oil in a wok or saucepan. Coat each piece of meat with the flour and deep-fry for 3 minutes. Remove the wok or saucepan from the heat but leave the meat in the oil for a further 2 minutes, then lift it out with a slotted spoon. Heat the oil again. Re-fry the meat with the bamboo shoots for 2 minutes or until they are golden, then remove and drain.

Pour off the excess oil, leaving about 1 tablespoon in the wok or frying pan. Add the spring onion and the green pepper, then the sweet and sour sauce mixture and stir until the sauce thickens and reduces. Add the pork and the bamboo shoots, blend well and serve hot.

Serves 4

Pork and Mixed Vegetables (Chop Suey)

This is a basic recipe for cooking pork, chicken, beef or prawns with vegetables (usually several different kinds, which can be varied according to seasonal availability). It is also an excellent way of using a few leftover vegetables.

250 g (8 oz) pork fillet, chicken or beef steak
2 tablespoons soy sauce
1 tablespoon dry sherry
2 teaspoons cornflour
125 g (4 oz) fresh bean sprouts
5 tablespoons oil
2 spring onions, cut into 2.5 cm (1 inch) lengths
1 slice fresh root ginger, peeled and finely chopped
1 small green pepper, cored and deseeded and cut into small pieces
a few cauliflower or broccoli florets, cut into small pieces
2–3 tomatoes, peeled and cut into small pieces
1–2 carrots, peeled and cut into small pieces
50 g (2 oz) green beans, cut into short lengths
2 teaspoons salt
1 tablespoon sugar
3 tablespoons beef or chicken stock

Cut the meat into small slices not much bigger than a postage stamp. Mix together the soy sauce, sherry and cornflour, and stir in the meat until each slice is well coated with the mixture.

Wash the bean sprouts in a basin of cold water, discarding the husks and any little bits that float to the surface of the water.

Heat about half the oil in a wok or frying pan and then stir-fry the meat slices for about 1 minute, stirring constantly, then remove the meat from the pan with a slotted spoon and set aside.

Heat the remaining oil, add the spring onions and ginger, then the rest of the vegetables and the salt and sugar. Stir for about 1 minute and add the meat. Blend everything well and moisten with a little stock if necessary.

Serve with boiled rice.

Serves 4

left: pork and mixed vegetables
right: pork in bean sauce

Stir-fried Bean Curd with Pork and Cabbage

Small holes may be left in the bean curd after thawing; these permit the delicious juices to penetrate. Do not freeze the bean curd for more than 12 hours or it will toughen.

1 bean curd (tofu) cake
250 g (8 oz) lean pork
3 tablespoons vegetable oil
1 spring onion, chopped
2 slices fresh root ginger, peeled and chopped
2 teaspoons salt
1 tablespoon dry sherry
1 litre (1¾ pints) chicken stock
500 g (1 lb) Chinese cabbage, shredded

Cut the bean curd into 3.5 cm (1½ inch) squares. Freeze overnight. Thaw in hot water, then drain.

Cut the pork roughly into small bite-sized pieces.

Heat the oil in a saucepan. Add the pork, spring onion, ginger and bean curd and stir-fry until the meat is lightly browned. Add the salt, sherry and stock and bring to the boil. Cover and simmer gently for 10 minutes.

Add the cabbage and simmer for about 10 minutes until just tender. Serve hot.

Serves 4–6

Pork in Bean Sauce

This is a very succulent dish. To save time, ask your butcher to chop the meat into small pieces for you.

1 tablespoon soy sauce
2 tablespoons dry sherry
1 tablespoon sugar
1 tablespoon plain flour
500 g (1 lb) pork spare ribs
3 tablespoons oil
1 garlic clove, crushed
2 spring onions, cut into 2.5 cm (1 inch) lengths
2 tablespoons crushed black or yellow bean sauce
5 tablespoons chicken stock or water
1 small green pepper, cored and deseeded and finely sliced
1 small red pepper, cored and deseeded and finely sliced

Mix together the soy sauce, sherry, sugar and flour. Add the chopped spare ribs and leave the mixture to marinate for about 10–15 minutes.

Heat the oil in a wok or frying pan and stir-fry the spare ribs until golden, then remove with a slotted spoon. Next, add the crushed garlic, the spring onions and the crushed black or yellow bean sauce to the wok or frying pan and stir gently. Add the spare ribs and blend well.

Add a little stock or water, place a lid on the wok or frying pan and cook over a high heat for 5 minutes. Add a little more stock or water if necessary, then replace the lid and cook for a further 5 minutes. Finally, add the green and red peppers, stir a few more times and serve hot.

Serves 4

Egg Fu-Yung

2 Chinese dried mushrooms or
   50 g (2 oz) fresh mushrooms
25 g (1 oz) cooked prawns, peeled
25 g (1 oz) ham
25 g (1 oz) bamboo shoots
2–3 water chestnuts
4 eggs, beaten
1 tablespoon cornflour
50 ml (2 fl oz) water
1 teaspoon salt
1 tablespoon sherry
3 tablespoons oil
To garnish:
cucumber twist
radish flowers

Soak the dried mushrooms in warm water for about 20 minutes, then squeeze dry and discard the hard stalks. Finely chop the mushrooms, prawns, ham, bamboo shoots and water chestnuts. Mix together with the beaten eggs. Add the cornflour, water, salt and sherry to the egg mixture and stir well to combine all the ingredients.

Heat the oil in wok or frying pan until smoking, then pour in the egg mixture and scramble with a fork until the mixture sets. Transfer to a warmed serving dish and garnish with the cucumber and radish.

Serves 4–6

Chow Mein

250 g (8 oz) egg noodles
300 g (10 oz) pork fillet
2 teaspoons cornflour
125 g (4 oz) bamboo shoots
125 g (4 oz) spinach leaves
½ cucumber
5 tablespoons oil
Sauce:
2 tablespoons soy sauce
1 tablespoon dry sherry
1 teaspoon salt
1 teaspoon sugar
1 teaspoon cornflour
1 teaspoon sesame seed oil,
   to garnish

Bring a saucepan of water to the boil, add the noodles and simmer for five minutes until soft but not sticky. Drain in a sieve and rinse with cold water.

Cut the pork into matchstick pieces and mix with the cornflour.

Cut the bamboo shoots, spinach and cucumber into thin shreds the same size as the pork.

Heat about half the oil in a wok or frying pan. Place the noodles in a large bowl, separating them with a fork, then pour over the hot oil.

Stir to ensure the noodles are evenly coated in the oil. Return them to the wok or pan and stir-fry for about 2–3 minutes. Transfer the noodles to a warmed serving dish with a slotted spoon.

Heat the remaining oil in the wok or pan and stir-fry the bamboo shoots, cucumber, spinach, pork and cornflour. Mix together the sauce ingredients and pour into the pan. Cook for about 2 minutes, stirring occasionally, then pour the mixture over the noodles. Garnish with a drizzle of sesame seed oil and serve hot.

Serves 4

Spring Rolls

125 g (4 oz) pork fillet
1 tablespoon soy sauce
1 tablespoon cornflour
125 g (4 oz) cooked prawns, peeled
1 egg white
250 g (8 oz) fresh bean sprouts
4 spring onions
3 tablespoons oil, plus extra for frying
1 tablespoon salt
6 eggs or 12 spring roll skins
about 2 tablespoons flour and water
    paste, for sticking
1 litre (1¾ pints) oil, for deep-frying

Finely shred the pork into thin slivers. Mix the soy sauce in a bowl with 1 teaspoon of the cornflour, add the pork and leave to marinate for about 20 minutes.

Coarsely chop the prawns. Mix the egg white with the remaining cornflour in another bowl. Stir in the prawns, cover and chill in the refrigerator until needed.

Wash and rinse the bean sprouts in a basin of cold water, discarding the husks and other bits and pieces that float to the surface.

Cut the spring onions into 2.5 cm

(1 inch) lengths and slice them into fine matchsticks.

Heat 2 tablespoons of the oil in a wok or frying pan and stir-fry the pork and prawns for 1 minute. Remove them with a slotted spoon and set aside. Heat the remaining oil in the pan until smoking, then stir-fry the bean sprouts and spring onions. Add the salt, followed by the pork and prawns. Stir constantly for about 1–2 minutes. Lift them out of the pan with a slotted spoon and set aside.

If using eggs, beat them well. Lightly grease the pan with oil. Place it over a low heat and pour in 2 tablespoons of beaten egg. Tip the pan from side to side until a thin, round pancake forms. Transfer gently with a fish slice to a warm plate. Continue until you have made 12 pancakes.

Place about 3 tablespoons pork and prawn filling on each spring roll pancake. Fold up the sides to make a tight roll and stick down the outer edges with a little flour and water paste.

Heat the oil in a wok or saucepan suitable for deep-frying and deep-fry the spring rolls a few at a time until golden. Crisp them in hot oil once more just before serving. Serve with a small bowl of soy sauce for dipping, if liked.

Serves 4

left: egg fu-yung
above: spring rolls

Noodles with Meat and Vegetables

Similar to Chinese chow mein, this dish can be prepared with meat and seafood of your choice.

250 g (8 oz) noodles
4 tablespoons oil
1 garlic clove, crushed
250 g (8 oz) boned lean pork, thinly sliced
250 g (8 oz) chicken breast meat, thinly sliced
250 g (8 oz) cooked, peeled prawns, deveined and diced
1 medium onion, thinly sliced
125 g (4 oz) shredded cabbage
2 tablespoons fish sauce
175 ml (6 fl oz) chicken stock
pinch of paprika
½ teaspoon salt
freshly ground black pepper
To garnish:
2 hard-boiled eggs, quartered
2 spring onions, chopped
few lemon wedges

Cook the noodles in a pan of boiling water for about 2 minutes until slightly cooked. Drain, rinse under cold running water, then drain again. Place in a bowl with 1 tablespoon of the oil and mix.

Heat 1 tablespoon of the oil in a wok. Add the noodles and fry until golden brown on all sides, then remove from the wok.

Wipe the wok clean with kitchen paper, then add 1 tablespoon of the oil and the garlic. Fry until the garlic is brown, then add the pork and fry for 5 minutes. Add the chicken and prawns and stir-fry for 2 minutes over high heat. Remove all the ingredients from the wok and set aside.

Wipe the wok clean again with kitchen paper and place over a high heat. When it is very hot, add the remaining oil, then the onion and cabbage. Stir-fry for about 4 minutes until the onion is just translucent but the cabbage is still slightly undercooked and crunchy.

Add the remaining ingredients, stir well, then add the cooked meat and fish mixture. Heat through for 2 minutes until most of the juices have evaporated, stirring constantly.

Add the noodles to the wok, toss well and cook until heated through. Pile on to a warmed serving dish. Garnish with the eggs, spring onions and lemon. Serve hot.

Serves 4–6

Pork Meatballs with Vegetables

500 g (1 lb) pork, not too lean
2 tablespoons soy sauce
1 tablespoon dry sherry
1¼ teaspoons sugar
1 egg
1 tablespoon cornflour
3–4 Chinese dried mushrooms
125 g (4 oz) transparent noodles
3 tablespoons oil
2 slices fresh root ginger, peeled and finely shredded
2 spring onions (white parts only), finely shredded
250 g (8 oz) Chinese cabbage or other greens, cut into small pieces
1 teaspoon salt
3 tablespoons chicken stock or water

Finely mince or chop the pork, then mix it with the soy sauce, sherry, sugar, egg and cornflour. Divide the mixture into 12, flour your hands, and roll the mixture into balls. Refrigerate until needed.

Soak the mushrooms in warm water for about 20 minutes, then squeeze dry and discard the hard stalks. Soak the transparent noodles until soft.

Heat the oil in a wok or frying pan and stir-fry the meatballs over a moderate heat until golden brown then remove with a slotted spoon. Add the ginger and spring onions to the wok, followed by the cabbage and mushrooms, and stir-fry.

Add the salt, stir, then add the meatballs and the noodles. Moisten with a little stock or water if necessary and bring to the boil. Reduce the heat, cover and simmer gently for about 20–25 minutes. Serve with boiled rice.

Serves 4

right: pork meatballs with vegetables

Stir-fried Beef with Onions

500 g (1 lb) rump steak
1 tablespoon dry sherry
½ teaspoon salt
2 tablespoons soy sauce
1 teaspoon sugar
4 tablespoons vegetable oil
2–3 slices fresh root ginger, peeled and shredded
1 large onion, thinly sliced
3 garlic cloves, crushed
1½ teaspoons cornflour, blended with 3 tablespoons beef stock
black pepper

To garnish:
tomato wedges (optional)
shredded spring onion

Cut the steak, against the grain, into thin pieces. Mix the sherry, salt, soy sauce, sugar, 1½ teaspoons of the oil and pepper to taste in a shallow dish. Add the steak and leave to marinate for 15 minutes.

Heat 2½ tablespoons of the remaining oil in a wok or frying pan over high heat. Add the ginger and onion and stir-fry for 1½ minutes. Push them to one side and add the remaining oil to the other side of the pan.

When the oil is very hot, add the steak and garlic to the pan and stir-fry for just a few seconds until brown. Mix in the chopped onion and shredded ginger and stir-fry for about 1 minute.

Stir in the blended cornflour mixture and cook, stirring, for about 30 seconds or until the sauce has thickened.

Garnish with tomato wedges, if using, and shredded spring onion and serve immediately.

Serves 4

below left: stir-fried beef with broccoli
below right: beef and mangetout

Stir-fried Beef with Broccoli

250 g (8 oz) lean rump steak, thinly
    sliced
2 teaspoons salt
2 teaspoons rice wine or dry sherry
1 tablespoon cornflour
4 tablespoons oil
250 g (8 oz) broccoli, divided into
    small florets
a little chicken stock or water
    (optional)
2 spring onions, cut into 2.5 cm
    (1 inch) lengths
125 g (4 oz) button mushrooms, sliced
1 tablespoon soy sauce

Cut the beef into narrow strips. Put
them into a bowl with ½ teaspoon of
the salt, the wine and cornflour and
mix well. Cover and leave to
marinate for 20 minutes.

Heat 2 tablespoons of the oil in a
wok and stir-fry the broccoli with
the remaining salt for a few
minutes, adding a little stock or
water to moisten if necessary.
Remove the broccoli and drain.

Heat the remaining oil in the wok
and fry the spring onions for a few
seconds. Add the beef and stir-fry
until evenly browned. Stir in the
mushrooms, soy sauce and broccoli.
Heat through and serve hot.

Serves 4

Beef and Mangetout

250 g (8 oz) rump steak, thinly sliced
2 tablespoons oyster sauce
1 tablespoon rice wine or dry sherry
1 teaspoon cornflour
4 tablespoons oil
2 spring onions, cut into 2.5 cm
    (1 inch) lengths
1 slice fresh root ginger, peeled and
    cut into strips
250 g (8 oz) mangetout, trimmed
1 tablespoon salt
1 teaspoon sugar

Cut the beef slices into narrow
strips and place them in a bowl
with the oyster sauce, rice wine
and cornflour. Mix well, then cover
and leave the meat to marinate for
about 20 minutes.

Heat 2 tablespoons of the oil in a
wok and stir-fry the spring onions
and ginger for a few seconds. Add
the beef and stir-fry until the meat
is evenly browned. Transfer the
mixture to a warmed serving dish
and keep hot.

Heat the remaining oil in the wok
and stir-fry the mangetout, salt and
sugar for about 2 minutes. (Be
careful not to overcook the
mangetout or they will lose their
crunchy texture and bright colour.)
Add the mangetout to the beef and
mix together well. Serve hot with
boiled white rice, if liked.

Serves 4

Beef with Green Peppers in Cantonese Black Bean Sauce

Though pork is undoubtedly the most popular meat in China, beef is an important part of the daily diet of the Chinese Moslems, who are widely distributed throughout China.

250–300 g (8–10 oz) beef frying steak
¼ teaspoon salt
1 tablespoon soy sauce
1 tablespoon rice wine or dry sherry
1 teaspoon sugar
1 tablespoon cornflour
125 g (4 oz) green pepper, cored and deseeded
125 g (4 oz) onions
2 slices fresh root ginger, peeled
2 spring onions
1–2 green or red chillies
4 tablespoons oil
1½ tablespoons salted black beans crushed in 1 tablespoon rice wine or dry sherry
To garnish:
spring onion flower
cucumber slice (optional)

Cut the beef into thin slices, then mix them with the salt, soy sauce, wine or sherry, sugar and cornflour.

Slice the green peppers and onions into small pieces. Cut the ginger, spring onions and chillies into thin shreds.

Heat the oil in a preheated wok or frying pan until smoking. Stir-fry the beef slices for a few seconds, then remove with a slotted spoon. Add the ginger, spring onions, chillies, green pepper and onion to the same oil. Stir a few times, then add the crushed black bean mixture and beef and blend together well. Cook for just 1 minute and serve immediately, garnished with a spring onion flower and cucumber, if liked.

Serves 4

Variation: Black bean sauce can be bought at supermarkets but it will not have the same fresh flavour as the crushed bean and wine mixture.

Dry-fried Sichuan Shredded Beef

Dry-frying is a cooking method that is unique to Sichuan cuisine. Its primary distinctive feature is that the main ingredients are first slowly stir-fried over a low heat with a variety of seasonings, then finished off with other ingredients stir-fried quickly over a high heat.

300 g (10 oz) beef frying steak
125 g (4 oz) carrots
2 tablespoons sesame seed oil
2 tablespoons rice wine or dry sherry
1 tablespoon chilli bean paste
1 tablespoon hoisin sauce or barbecue sauce
1 garlic clove, crushed and finely chopped
½ teaspoon salt
1 tablespoon sugar
2 spring onions, finely chopped
2 slices fresh root ginger, peeled and finely chopped
½ teaspoon freshly ground Sichuan or black pepper
1 teaspoon chilli oil

Cut the beef and carrots into fine matchstick pieces.

Heat the wok or frying pan over a high heat, add the sesame seed oil, then let it cool a little. Add the beef with 1 tablespoon of the wine or sherry. Stir until the pieces are separated, then reduce the heat. Pour off the excess liquid and continue stirring gently until the beef is absolutely dry. Next, add the chilli bean paste, hoisin or barbecue sauce, garlic, salt, sugar and the remaining wine or sherry. Stir a few times more.

Increase the heat to high, add the carrot pieces, stirring continually; then the spring onions, ginger, Sichuan or black pepper and chilli oil. Blend well and serve hot.

Serves 4–6

*top right: dry-fried sichuan shredded beef; **bottom right:** beef with green peppers in cantonese black bean sauce; **far right:** cantonese beef in oyster sauce*

Cantonese Beef in Oyster Sauce

250–300 g (8–10 oz) beef frying steak

1 teaspoon salt

½ teaspoon freshly ground pepper

1 teaspoon sugar

1 tablespoon light soy sauce

2 tablespoons rice wine or dry sherry

1 tablespoon cornflour

1 egg

1 small Chinese cabbage

4 tablespoons oil

1 spring onion, finely chopped

2 slices fresh root ginger, peeled and
   finely chopped

1½ tablespoons oyster sauce

Cut the beef into small, thin slices.
Mix in a bowl with a pinch of salt,
pepper, sugar, soy sauce, wine or
sherry, cornflour and the egg. Cover
and marinate for 20–30 minutes.

Cut the Chinese cabbage leaves
into 2–3 pieces. Heat 2 tablespoons
of the oil in a preheated wok or
frying pan and stir-fry the cabbage
with the remaining salt. Stir for
about 1½–2 minutes until the leaves
become limp. Remove the greens
and place them on a serving dish.

Wipe clean the wok or pan, then
heat the remaining oil until hot.
Add the spring onion, ginger and
then the beef, stirring; add the
oyster sauce and blend well. Cook
for 1 minute. Serve on the cabbage,
garnished with a chilli flower.

Serves 4

Quick-fried Beef in Oyster Sauce

2 tablespoons oil

4 spring onions, chopped

2 garlic cloves, sliced

4 carrots, diagonally sliced

2 celery sticks, diagonally sliced

375 g (12 oz) rump or sirloin steak

125 g (4 oz) bean sprouts

1 tablespoon soy sauce

2 tablespoons dry sherry

3 tablespoons oyster sauce

salt

To garnish:

carrot flowers (optional)

celery leaves

Heat the oil in a wok or frying pan, add the spring onions and garlic and fry quickly for 30 seconds. Add the carrots and celery and stir-fry for 1 minute.

Cut the steak into thin slices and sprinkle with salt. Add to the wok and fry until browned on all sides. Stir in the bean sprouts, soy sauce, sherry and oyster sauce and cook for 2 minutes.

Spoon the mixture into a warmed serving dish and garnish with the carrot flower, if liked, and celery leaves to serve.

Serves 4–6

*above left: quick-fried beef in oyster sauce; **above right:** deep-fried beef slices; **right:** sichuan hot shredded beef*

Deep-fried Beef Slices

4 spring onions, chopped

a pinch of salt

1 tablespoon dry sherry

2.5 cm (1 inch) piece of fresh root ginger, peeled and finely chopped

1 tablespoon chilli sauce

1 chilli, deseeded and finely chopped

500 g (1 lb) rump steak

oil, for deep-frying

Batter:

4 tablespoons plain flour

a pinch of salt

1 egg

3–4 tablespoons water

To garnish:

coriander leaves

lemon wedges

Put the spring onions, salt, sherry, ginger, chilli sauce and chilli in a bowl and mix well. Cut the steak into thin slices and add to the marinade. Toss well, cover and leave to marinate for 20–25 minutes.

Meanwhile, make the batter. Sift the flour and salt into a bowl, break in the egg and beat well, adding water to make a smooth batter.

Heat the oil in a wok or deep-fryer. Dip the steak slices into the batter and deep-fry in the hot oil until golden brown. Drain thoroughly on kitchen paper.

Arrange the meat on a warmed serving dish and garnish with coriander and lemon wedges. Serve immediately, with soy sauce served separately, if liked.

Serves 4–6

Sichuan Hot Shredded Beef

500 g (1 lb) rump or frying steak
2 tablespoons cornflour
3 tablespoons oil
4 spring onions, chopped
2 celery sticks, sliced diagonally
4 carrots, sliced diagonally
2 tablespoons soy sauce
1 tablespoon hoisin sauce
3 teaspoons chilli sauce
2 tablespoons dry sherry
salt
To garnish:
carrot flowers (optional)
celery leaves

Cut the steak into 5 cm (2 inch) long thin slices. Toss the steak in the cornflour and season to taste with salt.

Heat the oil in a wok or deep frying pan, add the spring onions and fry for 1 minute. Add the meat slices and cook for 4 minutes, stirring, until the meat is lightly browned. Add the celery and carrots and cook for 2 minutes. Stir in the soy, hoisin and chilli sauces and the sherry. Bring to the boil and cook for 1 minute.

Arrange on a warmed serving dish, garnish with carrot flowers, if using, and celery leaves and serve.

Serves 4–6

Rapid-fried Lamb Slices

This dish must be cooked over the highest heat in the shortest possible time, otherwise the meat will not be tender and juicy.

250–300 g (8–10 oz) leg of lamb fillet

about 12 spring onions

4 tablespoons oil

1 tablespoon soy sauce

½ teaspoon salt

1 tablespoon rice wine or dry sherry

½ teaspoon freshly ground Sichuan or black pepper

2 teaspoons cornflour

1 garlic clove, crushed

1 tablespoon sesame seed oil

1 tablespoon vinegar

Trim all the fat from the lamb and cut it into very thin slices. Cut the spring onions in half lengthways, then slice them diagonally.

Marinate the meat and spring onions in 1 tablespoon of the oil, the soy sauce, salt, wine or sherry, pepper and cornflour.

Heat the remaining oil in a preheated wok or deep frying pan until smoking. Add the crushed garlic to flavour the oil, then the lamb slices and spring onions, stirring constantly over a high heat for a few seconds, and finally the sesame seed oil and vinegar. Blend well, then transfer to a warmed serving dish and serve hot.

Serves 4

Sautéed Lamb with Spring Onions

2 tablespoons soy sauce

½ teaspoon salt

1 tablespoon dry sherry

125 ml (4 fl oz) vegetable oil

250 g (8 oz) lean lamb, very thinly sliced

1 tablespoon red wine vinegar

1 tablespoon sesame seed oil

½ teaspoon ground Sichuan or black peppercorns

2 garlic cloves, crushed

250 g (8 oz) spring onions

Mix together 1 tablespoon of the soy sauce, the salt, sherry and 2 tablespoons of the vegetable oil. Add the lamb slices and leave to marinate for 5 minutes.

Mix the remaining soy sauce with the vinegar, sesame seed oil and pepper in a small bowl.

Heat the remaining oil in a wok or frying pan. Add the garlic and stir-fry for about 10 seconds. Add the meat and stir-fry until browned. Shred a few of the spring onions and set aside for garnish. Cut the remainder into 5 cm (2 inch) pieces and add to the pan with the vinegar mixture. Stir-fry for a few seconds. Transfer to a warmed serving dish and serve hot, garnished with the spring onions.

Serves 2–4

Stir-fried Lamb with Noodles

125 g (4 oz) transparent noodles

500 g (1 lb) very lean lamb

1 tablespoon oil

3 spring onions, finely chopped

2.5 cm (1 inch) piece fresh root
   ginger, peeled and finely chopped

2 garlic cloves, sliced

2 celery sticks, chopped

1 red pepper, cored, deseeded and
   sliced

2 tablespoons light soy sauce

2 tablespoons dry sherry

150 ml (¼ pint) lamb or beef stock

2 teaspoons sesame seed oil

To garnish (optional):

green chilli flowers

spring onion flowers

Soak the noodles in warm water for
10 minutes; drain. Cut the lamb
into thin slices.

   Heat the oil in a wok or frying
pan, add the spring onions, ginger
and garlic and stir-fry for 1 minute.
Add the celery and lamb and cook

for 2 minutes. Add the red pepper,
soy sauce and sherry and bring to
the boil. Stir in the stock and
noodles and simmer for 5 minutes.
Sprinkle with the sesame seed oil.

   Transfer to a warmed serving dish
and garnish with chilli and spring
onion flowers, if using. Serve hot.

Serves 4–6

left: rapid-fried lamb slices
above: stir-fried lamb with noodles

Tung-Po Lamb

750 g (1½ lb) very lean lamb

4 spring onions

250 g (8 oz) carrots

4 celery sticks

2 tablespoons oil

3 tablespoons soy sauce

4 tablespoons dry sherry

2 leeks, sliced

4 garlic cloves, thinly sliced

2 pieces fresh root ginger, peeled
   and shredded

1 teaspoon lightly crushed black
   peppercorns

2 teaspoons sugar

To garnish:

lemon slices

coriander leaves

Cut the lamb into thin slices and cut each spring onion into about 3 pieces. Slice the carrots and celery sticks diagonally.

Heat the oil in a wok or frying pan, add the lamb and brown on both sides. Lower the heat, add the carrots and celery, and stir-fry for 2 minutes. Stir in the soy sauce and sherry. Cover and cook for about 15 minutes, or until the vegetables are tender.

Stir in the leeks, garlic, spring onions and ginger and cook for 1 minute. Add the peppercorns and sugar; heat until the sugar dissolves.

Transfer to a warmed serving dish, garnish with lemon and coriander and serve immediately.

Serves 4–6

Steamed Meat Dumplings

Left-over dumplings can be reheated either by steaming for 5 minutes or by shallow-frying in a wok or frying pan with a little oil for 6–7 minutes.

625 g (1¼ lb) plain flour
4 teaspoons baking powder
250 ml (8 fl oz) water
Filling:
1 tablespoon dry sherry
3 tablespoons soy sauce
2 teaspoons sugar
1 teaspoon salt
1 tablespoon sesame seed oil
2 teaspoons finely chopped fresh root
  ginger
1 teaspoon cornflour
500 g (1 lb) pork, not too lean,
  minced

Sift the flour and baking powder in a mixing bowl. Add the water and knead well. Cover the bowl with a damp cloth and place a small plate over the top, then leave the dough to rise at room temperature for about 2 hours.

Mix the sherry, soy sauce, sugar, salt, sesame seed oil, ginger and cornflour in a bowl, add the pork and mix thoroughly.

Divide the dough in half evenly, place the two halves on a lightly floured surface and knead well. Make each half into a long sausage-like roll 5 cm (2 inches) in diameter. Use a knife to slice each roll into about 15 rounds. Flatten the rounds with the palm of your hand, then with a rolling pin and roll out each piece into a pancake about 7.5 cm (3 inches) in diameter.

Place 1 tablespoon of the filling in the centre of each pancake, gather the sides of the dough up around the filling to join at the top, then lightly twist the top of the dough to close up tightly.

Place a piece of wet muslin on a rack in a steamer. Arrange the dumplings about 1 cm (½ inch) apart on the muslin, cover and steam vigorously for 20 minutes.

Serve hot with a selection of dipping sauces.

Serves 4

Vegetarian and Vegetables

Mixed Vegetables

The most important point in selecting the various ingredients for this dish is the balance of contrasting colours, textures and flavours. If, because of seasonal availability, some fresh vegetable substitutes have to be made, make sure they go well together.

3–4 Chinese dried mushrooms
50 g (2 oz) bamboo shoots
50 g (2 oz) fresh bean sprouts
50 g (2 oz) mushrooms
50 g (2 oz) mangetout or French beans
50 g (2 oz) broccoli or cauliflower
50 g (2 oz) carrots
4 tablespoons oil
1 tablespoon sugar
1 tablespoon soy sauce
2 teaspoons salt
1 tablespoon cornflour
2 teaspoons sesame seed oil

Soak the dried mushrooms in a bowl of water for about 25 minutes, then squeeze dry the mushrooms and discard the hard stalks. Cut into small pieces.

Cut the bamboo shoots into small bite-size slices.

Wash the bean sprouts in a basin of cold water, discarding the husks and other bits and pieces that float to the surface.

Chop the remaining vegetables into pieces roughly of the same size.

Heat about half of the oil in a wok or frying pan and stir-fry the dried mushrooms, bamboo shoots and bean sprouts, for only about 1 minute. Add half of the sugar, half of the soy sauce and half the salt, stir for a little while, then remove with a slotted spoon and set the mixture aside.

Wipe clean the wok or pan, heat the remaining oil and stir-fry the remaining fresh vegetables. Add the remaining salt and sugar and cook for about 1½ minutes, then mix in the parcooked vegetables. Cook together for a few seconds, then pour in the cornflour combined with a little water and the remaining soy sauce. Blend all the ingredients together. Add the sesame seed oil and serve either hot or cold.

Serves 4

Sweet and Sour Cabbage

3 tablespoons oil

5 dried hot chillies

12 peppercorns

500 g (1 lb) white cabbage, thinly
    shredded

1 green pepper, cored and deseeded
    and thinly sliced

1 red pepper, cored and deseeded
    and thinly sliced

1 tablespoon sesame seed oil, to
    garnish

Sweet and Sour Sauce:

2 tablespoons soy sauce

2 tablespoons vinegar

2 tablespoons sugar

1 teaspoon salt

Mix together all of the ingredients
for the sweet and sour sauce.

Heat the oil in a wok or large
frying pan and add the dried chillies
and peppercorns. After a few
seconds, add the cabbage and the
green and red peppers, stir for about
1–1½ minutes, then pour in the
sauce and continue stirring until
well blended.

Serve hot or cold, garnished with
sesame seed oil.

Serves 4

*far left: mixed vegetables; left: sweet
and sour cabbage; above: spicy
vegetables with noodles*

Spicy Vegetables with Noodles

Composite vegetable dishes like this can
be served as a meal on their own for a
light lunch or a snack and also make an
ideal accompaniment for meat dishes.

1.2 litres (2 pints) water

200 g (7 oz) cellophane or egg
    noodles

8 medium dried shiitake mushrooms

3 tablespoons sunflower oil

250 g (8 oz) Chinese cabbage,
    shredded

1 large carrot, thinly sliced

125 g (4 oz) spinach leaves, cooked
    and chopped

salt

Sauce:

1 tablespoon sesame oil

1 tablespoon soy sauce

2 teaspoons sugar

2 teaspoons sesame seeds

½ teaspoon salt

Bring the water to the boil in a
saucepan, add the noodles and boil
for 3 minutes, or according to
packet instructions. Drain well and
set aside.

Soak the mushrooms in boiling
water for 20 minutes. Drain well,
discard the hard stems and set the
caps aside.

Heat 2 tablespoons of the oil in a
saucepan, add the cabbage and salt
to taste and fry for 2 minutes.
Remove from the pan and set aside.
Heat the remaining oil in the pan
and stir-fry the carrot for 1 minute.
Return the cabbage to the pan, add
the spinach and mushrooms and
stir-fry for 2 minutes.

To make the sauce, put all the
ingredients into a saucepan over a
moderate heat and stir well. Bring
the sauce to the boil, then pour it
over the vegetables. Add the
noodles and toss well to combine.
Heat through and serve hot.

Serves 4

Stir-fried Ginger Broccoli

Ginger and broccoli make a wonderful partnership, which nicely offsets the oiliness of certain fish. Try it with red mullet, herring or mackerel recipes.

500 g (1 lb) broccoli
2 tablespoons sunflower oil
1 garlic clove, thinly sliced
2.5 cm (1 inch) piece fresh root
   ginger, peeled and finely shredded
½–1 teaspoon sesame oil
salt

*left: crispy seaweed with almonds;
below: stir-fried ginger broccoli; right:
mixed mushrooms in oyster sauce*

Crispy Seaweed with Almonds

The very popular seaweed served in Chinese restaurants is, in fact, green cabbage. (Real seaweed is found in Japanese cooking.) Choose fresh young spring greens with pointed heads which have not developed an ear. Often served as a starter, this recipe also makes an ideal garnish for a number of dishes, particularly cold starters.

750 g (1½ lb) spring greens
oil, for deep-frying
1 teaspoon salt
1½ teaspoon caster sugar
50 g (2 oz) deep-fried split almonds,
   to garnish

Wash and dry the spring greens and shred them with a sharp knife to give the thinnest possible shavings. Spread them out on kitchen paper or put them into a colander until dried thoroughly.

Heat the oil in a wok or deep-fryer, but before it gets too hot, turn off the heat for 30 seconds. Add the spring greens in several batches and turn the heat up to moderately high. Stir, and when the shreds start to float to the surface, scoop them out gently with a slotted spoon and drain on kitchen paper, removing as much of the oil as possible.

Sprinkle the salt and caster sugar evenly on top; then mix gently. Serve cold, garnished with almonds

Serves 4

Separate the broccoli heads into small florets. Peel the stems and slice them diagonally. Blanch quickly in lightly salted boiling water for 30 seconds, drain well and cool rapidly under cold running water; then drain thoroughly.

Heat the oil in a large wok or a frying pan over moderate heat and stir-fry the garlic and ginger for 3 seconds. Add the broccoli and cook for 2 minutes. Sprinkle over the sesame oil and stir-fry for a further 30 seconds. Spoon the broccoli into a warmed serving dish and serve at once.

Serves 4

Mixed Mushrooms in Oyster Sauce

50 g (2 oz) small dried Chinese mushrooms
2 tablespoons oil
4 spring onions, chopped

150 ml (¼ pint) vegetable stock
250 g (8 oz) straw mushrooms, washed and drained
125 g (4 oz) button mushrooms, washed and drained
3 tablespoons oyster sauce
1 tablespoon dry sherry

Soak the dried mushrooms in warm water for 15 minutes. Drain well and squeeze dry, then discard the hard stalks.

Heat the oil in a wok or deep frying pan, add the spring onions and stir-fry for 30 seconds. Add the mushroom caps and pour over the stock. Simmer for 15–20 minutes, until the mushrooms are tender.

Add the straw mushrooms and button mushrooms and cook for 1 minute. Pour over the oyster sauce and sherry, stir well and cook for about 2 minutes.

Pile the mixture into a warmed serving dish and serve immediately.

Serves 4–6

Stir-fried Mixed Vegetables

3½ tablespoons vegetable oil
1 onion, thinly sliced
3 garlic cloves, crushed
½ teaspoon salt
½ green pepper, cored, deseeded and sliced
½ red pepper, cored, deseeded and sliced
¼ cucumber, chopped
2 celery sticks, chopped
2 spring onions, chopped
3–4 lettuce leaves, chopped
250 g (8 oz) bean sprouts
1½ teaspoons sugar
2 tablespoons soy sauce
2 tablespoons vegetable stock

Heat the oil in a wok or deep frying pan, add the onion, garlic and salt and stir-fry for 30 seconds. Add all the remaining vegetables and toss until well coated. Sprinkle in the sugar, soy sauce and stock. Stir-fry for 1½ minutes. Serve hot.

Serves 2–4

Family-style Bean Curd

4 bean curd (tofu) cakes

4 tablespoons oil

125 g (4 oz) pork fillet, sliced into fine matchsticks

5–6 dried red chillies, finely chopped

1 leek, cut diagonally into bite-size chunks

1 tablespoon sherry

1 tablespoon soy sauce

2 tablespoons crushed yellow bean sauce

1 teaspoon sesame seed oil

Cut each bean curd cake crossways into 3 thin slices, then cut each slice diagonally into 2 triangles.

Heat 3 tablespoons of the oil in a wok or frying pan until hot, then fry the bean curd pieces for about 2 minutes, turning once. Remove with a slotted spoon and drain on kitchen paper.

Add the remaining oil and the pork, red chillies, and leek; stir-fry quickly. Add the sherry, soy sauce, bean curd and crushed bean sauce, and cook for about 3 minutes, then add the sesame seed oil and serve.

Serves 4

Fried Cauliflower

1 cauliflower

3 tablespoons oil

2 teaspoons salt

1 teaspoon sugar

4 tablespoons vegetable stock or water

sprig of parsley, to garnish (optional)

Wash the cauliflower in cold water, discarding the tough outer leaves and cut it into florets with part of the stalk still attached.

Heat the oil in a wok or deep frying pan and stir-fry the cauliflower for about 1 minute, then add the salt, sugar, vegetable stock or water. Cook for 2 minutes if you prefer the vegetables slightly underdone, otherwise cook for about 5 minutes, adding a little stock or water if necessary. Serve hot, garnished with parsley, as an accompaniment or as a light snack.

Serves 4

---

*left: family-style bean curd; **middle:** fried cauliflower; **right:** mushrooms in oyster sauce*

Mushrooms in Oyster Sauce

Just a few basic ingredients are needed to make this easy to prepare and delicious traditional dish.

3 tablespoons oil
500 g (1 lb) button mushrooms
2 tablespoons oyster sauce
2 teaspoons cornflour
2 tablespoons vegetable stock
1 teaspoon sesame seed oil
finely chopped parsley sprigs,
   to garnish

Heat the oil in a wok or frying pan and stir-fry the mushrooms for about 1½ minutes. Add the oyster sauce and continue cooking for about 1 minute.

Mix the cornflour to a paste with the vegetable stock and add to the mushrooms. When the gravy starts to thicken, add the sesame seed oil and blend well. Transfer to a warmed serving dish, garnish with finely chopped parsley and serve.

Serves 4

Chinese Vegetables

Water chestnuts are not nuts, but tubers which are peeled to reveal the white crisp flesh inside. Available in cans, once opened they will keep for two weeks, covered, in a refrigerator.

1 tablespoon sunflower oil
4 spring onions, chopped
250 g (8 oz) mangetout
250 g (8 oz) asparagus, cut into small
  pieces
125 g (4 oz) canned water chestnuts,
  drained and sliced
1 tablespoon light soy sauce
1–2 tablespoons rice wine or
  dry sherry
a pinch of salt
½ teaspoon sugar
1 teaspoon sesame oil

Heat the oil in a wok or deep frying pan over a moderate heat and stir-fry the spring onions for 3 seconds. Add the mangetout, asparagus and water chestnuts, toss well in the oil and cook for 1 minute. Add the soy sauce, wine or sherry, salt, sugar and sesame oil, and stir-fry for a further 3 minutes.

Transfer to a warmed serving dish and serve at once.

Serves 4

Celery Salad

1 celery stick, thinly sliced on the
  diagonal
1 small green pepper, cored,
  deseeded and thinly sliced
salt
1 slice fresh root ginger, peeled and
  finely shredded, to garnish
Dressing:
2 tablespoons soy sauce
1 tablespoon vinegar
1 tablespoon sesame seed oil

Place the celery and green pepper in a pan of lightly salted boiling water and blanch them quickly for about 1–2 minutes only. Transfer the

vegetables into a large colander and then rinse in cold running water until cool. Drain and transfer to a serving dish.

Mix together all the ingredients for the dressing and pour it over the celery and green pepper mixture. Toss well, then garnish the salad with the finely shredded ginger and serve immediately.

Serves 4

---

*left: chinese vegetables; **above left:** celery salad; **above right:** bean sprout salad*

Bean Sprout Salad

The Chinese seldom eat raw food, so typical salads consist of vegetables which are blanched, then cooled in cold water and mixed in a dressing.

500 g (1 lb) fresh bean sprouts
1 teaspoon salt
Dressing:
2 tablespoons soy sauce
1 tablespoon vinegar
1 tablespoon sesame seed oil
50 g (2 oz) finely sliced cooked ham
 or chicken, to garnish (optional)

Wash and rinse the bean sprouts in cold water, discarding the husks and other bits and pieces that float to the surface. (It is not necessary to top and tail each sprout.)

Place the bean sprouts in a pan of lightly salted boiling water and cook for 1–2 minutes only. Tip them into a colander and rinse in cold water until cool. Drain well, then transfer to a serving dish.

Mix together the ingredients for the dressing and pour it over the bean sprouts, stir and leave to stand for 10–20 minutes. Garnish with cooked ham or chicken if liked.

Serves 4

Braised Aubergines

The long, deep purple variety of aubergines are preferable to use for this recipe, if possible, rather than the large round ones.

600 ml (1 pint) oil, for deep-frying

300 g (10 oz) aubergines, cut into diamond-shaped chunks

2 tablespoons soy sauce

1 tablespoon sugar

2 tablespoons vegetable stock or water

1 teaspoon sesame seed oil

Heat the oil in a wok or saucepan until hot and then deep-fry the aubergine chunks in batches until golden, then remove with a slotted spoon and drain. Pour off the excess oil, leaving about 1 tablespoon in the wok.

Return the aubergines to the pan. Add the soy sauce, sugar and the stock or water. Cook for 2 minutes over a fairly high heat, adding more stock or water to moisten, if necessary and stirring occasionally. When the juice is reduced to almost nothing, add the sesame seed oil. Blend the mixture together well and serve hot.

Serves 4

above left: braised aubergines; ***above right:*** *aubergines in fragrant sauce;* ***right:*** *crispy vegetables*

Aubergines in Fragrant Sauce

250 g (8 oz) aubergines

125 g (4 oz) pork fillet

600 ml (1 pint) oil, for deep-frying

2 spring onions, finely chopped

1 slice fresh root ginger, peeled and finely chopped

1 garlic clove, finely chopped

1 tablespoon soy sauce

1 tablespoon sherry

2 teaspoons chilli purée

2 tablespoons cornflour

spring onion, chopped, to garnish

First, peel the aubergines, then cut them into small, bite-sized strips.

Then, cut the pork into matchsticks.

Heat the oil in a wok or saucepan and deep-fry the aubergine strips for 1–2 minutes. Remove with a slotted spoon and drain on kitchen paper.

Pour off the excess oil, leaving about 1 tablespoon in the wok and quickly stir-fry the spring onions, ginger and garlic, followed by the pork. Add the soy sauce, sherry and chilli purée, and blend well. Add the aubergine chips and cook together for 1–2 minutes. Combine the cornflour with a little water and pour it into the wok. Stir a few more times until the juice thickens, then serve hot, garnished with the chopped spring onion.

Serves 4

Crispy Vegetables

You can use many vegetables for this dish. Try cauliflower or broccoli florets, green beans, whole mushrooms, mangetout or strips of courgettes.

500 g (1 lb) mixed vegetables
oil, for deep-frying
Dip:
1–2 garlic cloves, chopped
4 tomatoes, skinned, deseeded and
  chopped

1 teaspoon chilli powder
2 avocado pears, peeled and stoned
1 tablespoon chopped coriander
  leaves
a pinch of ground coriander
Batter:
125 g (4 oz) plain flour
a pinch of salt
1 tablespoon sunflower oil
150 ml (¼ pint) water
2 egg whites, stiffly whisked

To make the dip, place all the ingredients in a blender and work to a smooth purée. Spoon into a dish and chill until required.

To make the batter, sift the flour and salt into a bowl. Gradually beat in the oil and water, then fold in the egg whites.

Heat the oil in a wok or frying pan to 180˚C (350˚F), or until a cube of day-old bread browns in 30 seconds. Dip the vegetables in the batter, then deep-fry in batches for 2–3 minutes until golden. Make sure the oil comes back to a high heat after each batch.

Drain the vegetables on kitchen paper and serve with the dip.

Serves 6

Chinese Fried Rice

The Chinese sausages used in this dish are available in Chinese stores and give an authentic flavour to this recipe.

500 g (1 lb) cold cooked rice (about 175 g (6 oz) uncooked)

6–8 tablespoons oil

1 egg, beaten

8 shallots or 2 small onions, sliced

3 garlic cloves, crushed

125 g (4 oz) cooked, peeled prawns, thawed if frozen

125 g (4 oz) Chinese sausage, sliced

125 g (4 oz) cold roast pork, shredded (optional)

4 dried Chinese mushrooms, soaked in warm water for 30 minutes, drained and sliced (optional)

1–2 tablespoons light soy sauce

125 g (4 oz) frozen peas, thawed

2 spring onions, sliced

1 red chilli, deseeded and chopped (optional)

coriander leaves

salt and pepper

To garnish:

shredded lettuce leaves

bay leaves (optional)

Cook the rice in a pan of boiling salted water until tender. Drain and leave until cold or cool overnight.

Heat a little of the oil in a frying pan and cook the egg to make an omelette. Roll it up into a sausage and cut it into fine strips. Set aside.

Heat 2 tablespoons of the oil in a wok and stir-fry the shallots or onions until crisp and golden brown. Lift out of the wok and reserve.

Add the garlic and prawns to the wok and cook for 1 minute, then set aside. Fry the Chinese sausage, shredded pork and mushrooms in the wok, then remove and reserve.

Heat sufficient oil in the wok to coat the rice completely. Stir-fry the rice for 2–3 minutes. Add the soy sauce, salt and pepper, plus half of the reserved cooked ingredients. Mix well, then add the peas and half the spring onions. Heat through for 3–4 minutes.

Serve the fried rice on a warmed serving platter and sprinkle with the remaining cooked ingredients, spring onions, the chilli and coriander leaves. Surround the rice with a garnish of shredded lettuce and bay leaves, if liked.

Serves 4–6

slotted spoon and set aside.

Heat the remaining oil in the pan, then add the remaining spring onions and cooked rice. Stir to separate each grain of rice. Add the soy sauce and stir until it is evenly blended with the rice, then add the eggs, ham, prawns and peas. Reduce the heat. Mix all the ingredients thoroughly and serve at once.

Serves 4

Vegetable Rice

2 tablespoons oil
2 leeks, sliced
2.5 cm (1 inch) piece fresh root
   ginger, peeled and finely chopped
1 garlic clove, sliced
250 g (8 oz) long-grain rice
250 g (8 oz) spring greens, shredded
salt

Heat the oil in a wok or deep frying pan. Add the leeks, ginger and garlic and fry for 30 seconds. Stir in the rice, covering all the rice with the oil mixture. Add boiling water to just cover the rice. Season to taste with salt. Bring to the boil, cover and simmer for 5 minutes. Add the greens, bring back to the boil and simmer for 7–9 minutes until the rice is just tender. Drain and serve.

Serves 4–6

left: chinese fried rice;
above left: *vegetable rice*

Easy Fried Rice

2 spring onions, finely chopped
3 eggs
1 teaspoon salt
4 tablespoons oil
50 g (2 oz) cooked ham, diced
50 g (2 oz) cooked, peeled prawns
125 g (4 oz) green peas
500 g (1 lb) cooked rice (about 175 g
   (6 oz) uncooked rice)
1½ tablespoons soy sauce

Mix half of the spring onions with the eggs, add a pinch of salt and beat lightly.

Heat a third of the oil in a wok or frying pan, then add the eggs and stir until scrambled. When the eggs set, transfer them to a warmed plate and break them into small pieces.

Heat another third of the oil in the pan. Place the ham cubes, the prawns, peas and the remaining salt in the pan and stir-fry quickly for about 1 minute then remove with a

Desserts

Deep-fried Sweet Potato Balls

500 g (1 lb) sweet potatoes
125 g (4 oz) rice flour
50 g (2 oz) soft brown sugar
125 g (4 oz) crystallized fruit,
   chopped
50 g (2 oz) sesame seeds, lightly
   toasted
oil, for deep-frying

Cook the potatoes in boiling water for 20 minutes until tender, drain and remove the peel. Mash the flesh and gradually beat in the flour and sugar. Stir in the crystallized fruit.

With dampened hands, roll the mixture into walnut-sized balls, then coat them with sesame seeds.

Heat the oil in a wok or deep-fryer and deep-fry the potato balls for 5–7 minutes, until golden brown. Drain on kitchen paper. Serve hot.

Serves 4–6

Walnut Sweet

125 g (4 oz) shelled walnuts
3 tablespoons oil
75 g (3 oz) dates, stoned
900 ml (1½ pints) water
150 g (5 oz) sugar
40 g (1½ oz) ground rice, blended
   with 3 tablespoons milk
apple flower, to decorate (optional)

Soak the walnuts in boiling water for 10 minutes, drain and remove the skins; dry on kitchen paper.

Heat the oil in a wok or deep frying pan, add the walnuts and fry quickly until lightly browned (take care not to burn them). Drain on kitchen paper.

Grind the nuts and dates in a food processor or blender. Bring the water to the boil and stir in the nut mixture, sugar and blended rice. Bring back to the boil, stirring, and cook for 2 minutes until thickened.

Spoon into a warmed serving dish. Decorate with an apple flower, if liked, and serve hot.

Serves 4–6

Steamed Cake

2 eggs
50 g (2 oz) brown sugar
75 ml (3 fl oz) milk
125 g (4 oz) self-raising flour
1 tablespoon lard or vegetable fat
golden syrup, to serve

Beat the eggs in a mixing bowl and stir in the sugar and milk. Fold in the sifted flour and mix together.

Melt the lard or vegetable fat, and when cool, add to the mixture.

Pour the cake mixture into a greased 20 cm (8 inch) cake tin and steam vigorously for 20–30 minutes.

Remove the cake from the tin while it is still hot. Divide it into squares or triangles and then serve it hot or cold with golden syrup.

Serves 4

left: deep-fried sweet potato balls
above: walnut sweet

Eight-treasure Rice Pudding

This is a festival dish traditionally served at New Year and other special occasions. The eight treasures are eight different dried fruits and nuts representing eight charms, which are said to ward off evil spirits. The recipe has been modified somewhat as some of the ingredients are unobtainable in the West.

250 g (8 oz) short-grain rice
3 tablespoons lard
3 tablespoons sugar
15 dried red dates
30 seedless raisins
10 walnuts
10 glacé cherries
1 tablespoon chopped candied
   angelica
Filling:
250 g (8 oz) can sweetened chestnut
   purée
Syrup:
3 tablespoons sugar
300 ml (½ pint) water
1 tablespoon cornflour

Wash the rice in cold water. Place it in a saucepan and add enough water to cover. Bring to the boil, then reduce the heat, cover and simmer very gently for 10–15 minutes or according to packet instructions.

Mix 2 tablespoons of the lard with the cooked rice and stir in the sugar.

Grease the bottom and sides of a 900 ml (1½ pint) mould or pudding basin with the remaining lard.

Cover the bottom and sides of the mould with a thin layer of cooked rice. Press a line of each fruit and nuts into this layer in a decorative pattern. Cover this with a layer of rice, then another layer of fruit and nuts. Cover with rice and layer with the remaining fruit and nuts, sandwiched between layers of rice. You will now have attractive rows of fruit and nuts around the edges with a hollow in the centre. Press gently to the sides of the mould so that the colours will show through when turned out for serving later on.

Cover the fruits and nuts with another layer of cooked rice, much thicker this time, then fill the centre with the chestnut purée and finally cover it with the rest of the rice. Press down gently to flatten the top.

Cover with foil and steam the pudding in a double boiler for about 1 hour.

Meanwhile, make the syrup. Dissolve the sugar in the water over gentle heat. When it has dissolved, increase the heat and boil for about 5 minutes. Thicken the syrup by stirring in the cornflour mixed with a little cold water.

Turn out the pudding on to a round dish, pour the syrup over it and serve hot.

Serves 4

Almond Fruit Salad

This is a delicious variation on the traditional fruit salad.

4 dessert apples, cored
4 peaches, skinned and stoned
125 g (4 oz) strawberries
4 slices of pineapple
125 g (4 oz) lychees, skinned
Almond Syrup:
2 tablespoons ground almonds
450 ml (¾ pint) water
1 tablespoon cornflour, blended with
  2 tablespoons water
3 tablespoons sugar

First, make the almond syrup. Put the almonds, water, blended cornflour and sugar in a pan and mix well. Gradually bring to the boil, stirring, then simmer for 10 minutes, stirring constantly. Remove from the heat and leave to cool, stirring the syrup occasionally to prevent a skin forming.

Slice the apples, peaches and strawberries; cut the pineapple into cubes. Put all the fruit into a bowl and mix well. Spoon over the almond syrup and chill well before serving.

Serves 4–6

left: almond junket
above: almond fruit salad

Almond Junket

This dessert is most refreshing to eat when served very cold.

150 ml (¼ pint) evaporated milk
600 ml (1 pint) water
25 g (1 oz) gelatine powder
4 tablespoons granulated sugar
1 teaspoon almond essence
300 g (10 oz) can mandarins or
  cherries

Put the milk and water into a saucepan over a very gentle heat. Add the gelatine and sugar and stir to dissolve. Add the almond essence then pour the mixture into a large serving bowl. Let it cool for at least 30 minutes then put it in the refrigerator for 3 hours to set.

To serve, cut the junket into small cubes, pour over the canned fruit and syrup.

Serves 4

Toffee Apples

4 large, firm dessert apples, peeled
   and cored
4 tablespoons plain flour
1 tablespoon cornflour
2 egg whites
1 litre (1¾ pints) oil, for deep-frying
125 g (4 oz) sugar
2 tablespoons water
1 tablespoon lard
1 tablespoon sesame seeds

Cut each apple into eight pieces.
Sprinkle the pieces with a little of
the flour. Mix the remaining flour
with the cornflour and egg whites
to make a batter. Heat the oil in a
wok or saucepan, coat each piece of
apple with batter, and deep-fry for
about 3 minutes. Remove the apple
pieces with a slotted spoon and
drain thoroughly on kitchen paper.

   Place the sugar and water in a
saucepan and stir over a gentle heat.
Add the lard, increase the heat and
continue stirring until the sugar has
caramelized. Add the apple pieces,
stir, and add the sesame seeds.
Blend well. Dip each piece of apple
into a bowl of cold water to harden
the toffee before eating. Serve as
soon as they are set.

Serves 4

left: toffee apples
right: *water chestnut cake;* ***far right:***
fruit custard

Toffee Bananas

The batter mixture for this recipe may be
prepared well in advance of cooking. It is
essential that the toffee-covered fruit is
dipped into the water while the toffee is
very hot. This is best done in the kitchen
before serving as it may be messy.

4 bananas
1 egg
2 tablespoons plain flour
600 ml (1 pint) oil, for deep-frying
4 tablespoons sugar
1 tablespoons water

Cut the bananas in half lengthwise,
then cut each half into two pieces.

   Beat the egg in a bowl, add the
flour and mix to make a batter. Heat
the oil in a wok or saucepan, coat
each piece of banana with batter
and deep-fry until golden. Remove
the banana with a slotted spoon
and drain thoroughly.

   Pour off the excess oil leaving
about 1 tablespoon oil in the wok or
saucepan. Add the sugar and water
and stir over a gentle heat to
dissolve the sugar.

   Increase the heat and when the
mixture becomes golden brown,
quickly mix in the banana pieces,
blending well. Dip each piece of
banana into a bowl of cold water in
order to harden the toffee coating.
Serve immediately.

Serves 4

Water Chestnut Cake

150 g (5 oz) water chestnut flour, sifted

350 ml (12 fl oz) water

500 g (1 lb) canned water chestnuts, well drained and chopped

50 g (2 oz) unsalted butter

150 ml (¼ pint) milk

250 g (8 oz) caster sugar

strawberry slices, to decorate

Put the flour into a bowl and gradually beat in the water to form a smooth batter.

Place the water chestnuts, butter, milk and sugar in a large pan and bring to the boil. Remove from the heat and stir in half the batter. Bring back to the boil, stirring. Remove from the heat and add the remaining batter. Return to the boil and cook, stirring, for 30 minutes.

Pour the batter into a lined and greased 18 cm (7 inch) square shallow cake tin and cover with greaseproof paper and foil, securing with string. Steam over high heat for 25–30 minutes until firm. Leave the cake to cool in the tin.

Turn out the cake and cut it into diamond shapes. Arrange them on a serving plate and decorate with strawberry slices.

Serves 4–6

Fruit Custard

3 eggs

4 tablespoons caster sugar

300 ml (½ pint) water

375 g (12 oz) pineapple

50 g (2 oz) dates

125 g (4 oz) crystallized fruit

25 g (1 oz) dried figs

1 tablespoon arrowroot or cornflour

Beat the eggs, 1 tablespoon of the sugar and 4 tablespoons of the water in a deep ovenproof dish. Place the dish in a steamer and steam for 7–8 minutes until the mixture is set.

Finely shred the pineapple, dates, crystallized fruit and figs. Mix together all the fruit and spoon over the egg custard.

Mix together the arrowroot or cornflour and remaining sugar. Gradually blend in the remaining water. Bring to the boil, stirring, and cook for 2 minutes. Spoon over the fruit and serve hot or cold.

Serves 4

Index